Edward Schillebeeckx:
In Search of the Kingdom of God

Edward Schillebeeckx
In Search of the Kingdom of God

JOHN BOWDEN

CROSSROAD · NEW YORK

1983
The Crossroad Publishing Company
575 Lexington Avenue, New York, N.Y. 10022

© John Bowden 1983

Printed in the United States of America

Library of Congress Cataloging in Publication Data

Bowden, John Stephen.
  Edward Schillebeeckx: in search of the kingdom of God.

  Bibliography: p. 155
  Includes index.
  1. Schillebeeckx, Edward, 1914-   . I. Title.
BX4705.S51314B68 1983   230'.2'0924   83-7866
ISBN 0-8245-0610-3 (pbk)

Contents

Acknowledgments   vi

Foreword by David Tracy   vii

Preface by Edward Schillebeeckx   xi

1   Introduction   1

2   Life   20

3   Christ the Sacrament   39

4   Jesus   55

5   Ministry   74

6   Salvation from God   90

7   Spirituality   104

8   Political Theology   117

9   'A Brief Hermeneutical Intermezzo'   130

10   Assessment – and the Future   141

Bibliography   155

Notes   157

Index   163

Acknowledgments

I owe a deep debt of gratitude to four people in particular over this book. Ton van der Worp, Managing Director of the Dutch publishing firm Ten Have, must have the most active photocopier in Holland, and over the past few years he has sent me a great deal of material from newspapers and periodicals which otherwise I would have missed completely. That is only one of his many kindnesses. It was through him that I came to meet Lucas Grollenberg, who introduced me to the Dutch Dominican Order and the Albertinum and opened my eyes to many things about which I had previously been blind; his own special kind of friendship has given me something that words cannot adequately express. Ted Schoof, for long the personal assistant of Edward Schillebeeckx, has provided some brilliant analyses of his theology and way of working without which my comments would have been very much thinner; these are duly acknowledged in the notes. He also read the first draft of this book and has much improved it by his perceptive comments. Finally, Edward Schillebeeckx has been his usual generous self in reading and correcting the text and writing the preface.

More formally, I must acknowledge permission to quote from the works of Edward Schillebeeckx. In Holland they are published by the firm of H. Nelissen, Baarn; in England by Sheed and Ward, Collins and SCM Press; in the United States by Sheed and Ward and Crossroad Publishing Company.

JOHN BOWDEN

Foreword

by David Tracy

It is a pleasure to introduce this fine and sensitive study of a great theologian. Few thinkers, in their own lifetimes, receive the kind of judicious and critical introduction they deserve. What a general audience needs for Schillebeeckx's thought is not another technical discussion of his terms and the several critical turns of his thought. That can and should be left to the journals. What we need, but up to now have not received, is a good, brisk 'heart of the matter' discussion of Schillebeeckx's religious vision and theological journey. Through John Bowden's unusual skills as editor, theologian, translator and critic, we finally receive exactly that.

To read John Bowden's sensitive portrait of Schillebeeckx is to recall the civilized pleasures of an older kind of cultural criticism. It is the pleasure of a good, even relaxed conversation. It is the pleasure of that essay genre which the British have long since perfected. It is, above all, the pleasure of a fine writer able to communicate his unfeigned yet critical delight in a greater writer's vision. It is the kind of enjoyment—and the peculiar kind of understanding that comes from such enjoyment—which happens when reading Isaiah Berlin on Vico or F. R. Leavis on D. H. Lawrence.

This kind of introduction was badly needed for Schillebeeckx's work. For Edward Schillebeeckx's long and fruitful theological journey has produced so many works and has responded to so many promptings that someone was needed to steer an interested but wary reader to the heart of the matter. This John Bowden does with great skill. He explores with care the heart of this representatively twentieth-century theological journey: from the first phenomenological and personalist theology of encounter and sacramentality through the magisterial works in christology, the courageous works on ministry, church reform and political theology to the work-in-progress on hermeneutics, the doctrine of the Spirit and the pressing question of world religions.

Schillebeeckx is unusual among contemporary theologians in his willingness, even eagerness, to learn new methods, study new disciplines, read new books and consult his own extraordinary knowledge of the whole history of theology for genuinely new insights. He seems less gripped by the intensity of a single vision of the whole than most theologians. And yet, for precisely that reason, Schillebeeckx calls for a guide to introduce his work to a wider readership.

What we have needed, in sum, is someone who can show us the central vision which perdures amidst all the changes, turns, wanderings and revisions. We want, to be sure, to know what the real changes were. This Bowden nicely does in his analysis of the radical differences between Schillebeeckx's earlier sacramental theology and his later work on christology, ministry and political theology. But we also want to be able to see the continuties. This Bowden does exceptionally well by showing the continuities between Schillebeeckx's early 'turn to the world' in his work with Chenu and the worker-priest movement and his later more radical turn to liberation and political theology. He suggests as well the continuity between Schillebeeckx's early De Petter-like version of phenomenology and encounter philosophy and his later method of 'mutually critical correlations' between contemporary experience and the great Judaeo-Christian tradition. Bowden also shows clearly how central the category of 'experience' as both subjective and objective has been for Schillebeeckx all along: as he moved from his earlier form of phenomenology to his later hermeneutics and his recent brilliant analysis of the 'contrast experience' of suffering. Bowden delineates with sensitivity and insight the kinds of differences which Schillebeeckx's Dominican spirituality has occasioned from his early work on Thomas Aquinas and Albert the Great to his most recent 'mystico-political' thought. Above all, Bowden leads his readers carefully and surely to the heart of the matter: Schillebeeckx's extraordinary confidence in and loyalty to the reality of God's grace for all humanity.

In reading Schillebeeckx one often has the impression of a theologian who will not shrink from facing any of the radically negative experiences of our frightening times, yet one who faces them with an enviably sturdy confidence in God, allied to a confidence that God *is for humanity.* Such confidence can often, in a Christian theologian, give rise to something approaching arrogance, even fanaticism. With Schillebeeckx, the amazement is that this never happens. The confidence never wavers but the arrogance never comes. Like the great Flemish and Dutch painters of his heritage, Schillebeeckx seems able to see life whole by seeing it in all its details, welcome and unwelcome ("About suffering they were never wrong, the old masters."—W. H. Auden). There is in this theology a steadiness of vision without heaviness, an experiential cast without a flouting of theory, a paradoxically earthy mysticism which lends itself in our time to contemporary praxis and to politics.

I admire Schillebeeckx's theology very much and I am thankful to John Bowden for helping me to see it more clearly and as a whole. Like Bowden, I, too, admire Edward Schillebeeckx as a person and am honored to hold him as a friend. It was once said of John Henry Newman that those who knew only his books knew the least part of him. A paradoxical thought, surely, given *those* book. I have no idea if that was true of Newman, but it is indeed true of Edward Schillebeeckx. His books, like Newman's, are lasting achievements. But his person—that steady, listening, searching and answering man—is the one John Bowden helps us all to see more clearly as the 'implied author' lurking in the books themselves.

Edward Schillebeeckx deserves John Bowden's tribute. And Bowden's book fully deserves the wide readership it should receive.

Preface

by Edward Schillebeeckx

This book by John Bowden differs from the several dozen doctoral dissertations which have been written about my theological work by being a pastoral-theological, evocative introduction to the work of a theologian. John Bowden does not analyse all my works, but with a sure hand grasps the main lines of my theological thinking, with the result that he is often better able to show readers what my books are really about than the heavily academic doctoral theses.

At its best, 'theology' is always a joint activity: doing theology with or sharing the thought of the theologian one seeks to introduce. That is what Bowden is doing in this book. He sets out to uncover the foundations of the hope which inspires my theological work, and generally does so with unerring accuracy; sometimes he even brings to light features of my work of which I have been unconscious, or which have not been completely clear.

The fact that in the English translations of some of my works subtle nuances of the Dutch original have escaped his notice does not seem to present any problems so far as this book is concerned. Bowden is less concerned to present all the details of my work than to demonstrate its inner dynamics. And in that respect he is thoroughly successful, sometimes in an amazing way.

In my view the Christian confession is about a historical phenomenon, Jesus of Nazareth, a particular man with a history of his own which ended in a crucifixion. This man is believed to have been a manifestation of God's action for the salvation of humankind. Jesus' understanding of God and his message of the kingdom of God are so integrated into his active, liberating dealings with men and women that his understanding of God, his proclamation and his life-style reciprocally interpret one another, while together they 'change' his followers and all who believe in him, making them new men and women. By his human concern for fellow human beings, in his human existence Jesus affirms and reveals God as a saving and liberating God.

Consequently I can understand Jesus only as one who in his human form brings us an understanding of God which is salvation, which brings liberation to men and women. In Christ we are given an answer to the question of God, and at the same time an answer to humankind's quest for salvation. Any christology which neglects the particular relationship to God in Jesus' concern for humankind or vice versa, misunderstands the specific character of Jesus' life and in so doing destroys both soteriology and christology. For me, the specific character of Jesus of Nazareth is made up of the intrinsic connection between the person of Jesus, his understanding of God, his career and message, and finally his execution in the form of a Roman crucifixion. This intrinsic bond between God and the man Jesus, focussed on human salvation, is endorsed for ever by the eschatological 'new act' of God which raised him from the dead.

All this presupposes that Jesus did indeed live in the awareness of being loved and accepted by God, even in his death, and moreover that he wanted his followers, those who believed in him, to share in that awareness of being completely accepted by God. Hence the 'Our Father'. Thus the church's affirmation that Jesus is 'the Son of God' has its deepest roots in the person and career of the man Jesus himself.

This book by John Bowden helps us clearly to feel something of the hope which Christians can derive from all this for their own lives, in good days and in bad.

1

Introduction

'What the Beatles are for us, you are for the Sisters who teach us,' said his nephew to Edward Schillebeeckx in 1968.[1] And that was at an early stage of his public recognition. When he was involved in an investigation of the orthodoxy of his teaching in 1979 after the publication of his book *Jesus*, he pointed to the tokens he had received without the slightest trace of immodesty and self-import-ance and remarked, 'I'm like a football star – all these flowers and gestures of support.' These are two spontaneous reactions to a man who might not have been expected to become so prominent in the media, whose main achievement is to have written long and difficult books and articles, and whose almost unpronouncable name outside his own language-area is current in two different forms (the inac-curate *Skillerbeeks* obstinately refusing to yield everywhere to the rather more accurate *Skillabakes*).

A good deal had happened between these two incidents. By 1968, Schillebeeckx, then in his fifties, had made a considerable reputation in Roman Catholic circles as a gifted creative theologian who had proved an invaluable adviser to the Dutch bishops and had done important interpretative and critical work on an unofficial basis during the Second Vatican Council. Above all, he was known for his fresh and imaginative reinterpretation of the sacraments, much influenced by existentialism, entitled *Christ the Sacrament of En-counter with God*. This book was talked about outside Catholic circles and had been translated into ten languages – and had not called forth the slightest criticism from official circles. It had made Schillebeeckx an international theologian's theologian, but other-wise, outside Holland he was far from being a household name in other church traditions or in the wider world. Even for his fellow

Catholics in Holland and Belgium his books and articles were not
the most approachable of reading, and the learning they displayed
made considerable demands on those who embarked on them.
However, because of his many appearances, giving lectures or
appearing on television, Schillebeeckx, an attractive and likeable
person, had shown that he had something important to say to men
and women in the modern world, and as time went on they found
that his books had about them a richness which made them worth
persevering with, even if this meant consulting reference works for
explanations of the technical terms and going through the text
several times. At that time his most accessible book was a fresh and
imaginative reinterpretation of the eucharist, much influenced by
existentialism and entitled *Christ the Sacrament of Encounter with
God*. It was talked about outside Catholic circles and translated into
German, French and English. With it, Schillebeeckx became an
international theologian's theologian, but otherwise, outside Holland was far from being a household name.

By 1979 much of this had changed. Thanks to the disclosure of the
investigation going on into the orthodoxy of some of the content of
his substantial book *Jesus* which had appeared in the meanwhile, in
circumstances the apparent injustice of which shocked the public
worldwide, Schillebeeckx had become a symbol, even to those who
were not church members, of the right of Catholic theologians to
study their subject freely in an academic setting. Because of a very
long delay in the appearance of an English translation of *Jesus*, the
exact details of the accusation were less well-known in Britain and
America than in Europe, but to the countless petitions started in
Holland and elsewhere, was added an unparalleled gesture: theologians representing virtually every theological faculty and depart-
ment in England and Scotland joined in a letter of protest to *The
Times*. Because over approximately the same period the German
theologian Hans Küng had also been involved in ongoing controversy with the church, 'Küng and Schillebeeckx' came to be linked
together as a pair of rebels allied in combatting the oppression of the
Vatican.

Schillebeeckx had now become a familiar name, but at a price.
He was publicized on the whole for what his opponents claimed that
he did not believe, rather than for his positive reinterpretation of
difficult doctrinal questions; his views were not allowed the

measured presentation they need if they are to be understood, but were assessed by criteria some of which to his way of thinking – and indeed that of virtually all other competent academic theologians – were outdated and inappropriate. The procedures of 'the New Inquisition' were outlined in detail, and a blow-by-blow account was given of the development of an affair which ended in anti-climax because of a still-unbroken subsequent silence on the part of the Vatican. So it is that when the name 'Schillebeeckx' is mentioned in non-theological circles, if it meets with recognition it will be in terms of, 'Oh, the dissident theologian'. And even those who have followed the case fairly closely may be hard put to recall what the whole business was about, apart, perhaps, from a vague memory of denials that Jesus was the Son of God or that the resurrection was a real event.

That would be a pity, for despite the problems they present – and they are very real ones – Edward Schillebeeckx's books are a unique contribution to modern theology, and not only for his fellow Catholics. His name deserves to stand alongside that of Karl Barth (with whom he has more in common; not least in personal charisma, than might appear possible at first glance) as being one of the very greatest theologians, not least – and this is the most important thing of all – in the sense of joy in believing which emerges so often in his theology.

Those who need persuading that his writings are worth the effort might do worse than open the very first page of *Jesus*, the beginning of a section on 'Why this book has been written'. They will find there, as at the beginning of *Christ*, a story from the Bible, in this case the healing by Peter, recorded in the Acts of the Apostles, of the lame man who sat begging for alms at the 'gate of the temple called Beautiful'.[2] So long is the investigation which follows, that by the end of the book one might be forgiven for forgetting just how it began. But the beginning is also the ending. Returning to this opening story, Schillebeeckx records how in the same vein Martin Buber has a rabbi relate a similar episode.

> My grandfather was paralysed. One day he was asked to tell about something that happened with his teacher – the great Baal-shem. Then he told how the saintly Baal-shem used to leap about and dance while he was at his prayers. As he went on with the story my

grandfather stood up; he was so carried away that he had to show how the master had done it, and started to caper about and dance. From that moment on he was cured. That is how stories should be told.[3]

And that is how theology should be done. Theology should be a joyful business, not needing any excuses. If his own book, Schillebeeckx goes on, helps towards the kind of believing that really counts; if it really achieves something because its basis is the abiding and appealing presence in the world of the kingdom of God and the praxis that goes with it, then he will count himself happy. If not, the book may as well be marked down and sold off to the remainder merchants.

Both the introduction of this vivid and attractive illustration and the perhaps unfamiliar word 'praxis' which appears in the following paragraph should hold our attention for a moment, as elements of the distinctive and initially disconcerting way in which Schillebeeckx goes about writing his theology. One of the features which make the Schillebeeckx writings a delight to read is the way in which, often after page after page of complicated theology, a simile is introduced, sometimes so bold and imaginative that it almost goes beyond itself and fails to come off. One sees what he is getting at and is almost carried away by the exuberance, shaking one's head at the audacity but at the same time warming to him and feeling with him, in a way which almost transcends any rational process, the reality which he is seeking to indicate.

There is an excellent example in *Christ the Sacrament*, in similar vein, where he is talking about the way in which Christ through his glorified body takes up material things of our human world into a dynamic unity with his risen and active body.

I hope I may be forgiven for drawing a likeness between the sacred sacramental event and present-day jazz, but perhaps the coherence of the sacramental whole can best be suggested by means of the image of a drummer. Just as when a drummer is playing he is extending himself through all his bodiliness into the instruments grouped about him, so that these instruments dynamically participate in the expressiveness of his rhythmic movement, making but one total movement which, arising from within the drummer, flows through the rhythm of his body, of his beating hands and stamping feet, and produces a varied harmony of percussion – so too the heavenly saving will of Christ, through his glorified body, makes one dynamic unity with the ritual gesture and the sacramental words of the minister who intends to do what the Church does.[4]

It would be misleading to suggest that Schillebeeckx's works are liberally sprinkled with illustrations of this kind, or that they play a major role in the presentation of his theology. But they are there, sometimes reduced to a single illuminating comment in which he suddenly becomes personal and informal, and are a significant element in the complex construction of his writings. We shall be looking at that in more detail shortly.

The word 'praxis', in fact a piece of theological jargon which has acquired rather more overtones in its usage than the almost synonymous 'practice' (as in 'Practise what you preach'), represents another important ingredient in the mix, perhaps the most important of all. A Dutch journalist writing in the journal *De Tijd* commented that when Schillebeeckx is talking about anything whatsoever, however informally, within five minutes he will have used the word 'praxis' three times or more, and of course his books are full of it.[5] This is because he feels that the activity of the creator God who is at work in human history can be traced above all in human action. By examining the nature of that action we can also explore what meaning there may be in life. If religion is concerned with our human existence or is an expression of the meaning of that existence, then while the question of this meaning may be avoided in theoretical discussions, it cannot be avoided when we come to human action. Although the emphases in Schillebeeckx's work have changed over the years and the church does not play quite the same role in them that it used to, having given way to Jesus and the kingdom of God, it is quite evident from beginning to end that one is not reading one of those theologians – and in fact there are all too many of them – for whom writing books and doing theology are something quite different from saying prayers and sharing in the practical and liturgical life of the church. Nor is there any polemic in his work – except sometimes against those who have failed to read him carefully enough before passing judgment on what he has written – which makes it such a pity that his name is so often coupled with that of

Hans Küng, who has seemed to delight in nothing more than argument with authority.

Edward Schillebeeckx is a Dominican, and a Dominican whose love of the Order is quite manifest, as, for example, when he describes its spirituality at length (we shall be looking at this later).[6] Worship is important for him; *Christ* comes to an end after nearly a thousand pages with a sermon, a creed, a canticle and prayers of thanksgiving,[7] and when in connection with the award to him of the Erasmus prize in 1982 a book was published based on almost twenty hours of conversation with two journalists, he brought it to a conclusion by writing a personal psalm[8] which is now widely in liturgical use in Holland. When asked by the same journalist whether he talked with God, he replied quite simply, 'Yes', and when pressed to expand the monosyllable explained that he had never had any difficulty in talking with God as with a friend. Perhaps the conversation had grown more critical than it had been when he was young, but the simple habit of talking with God had remained. 'You can only talk about God,' he concluded, 'when you've been talking with him.'[9] As time has gone on, a further dimension has developed in his theology. His growing realization of the limitations of the church in its present form and the demands of the Third World have made him realize that in our global circumstances praxis must also include political action and that the direction this action should take must also be reflected upon in political theology. That too we shall consider in more detail in due course.[10]

Before going further into the character of Schillebeeckx's writings, however, it would be as well to know precisely what we are talking about. There can be no question here of a complete listing of his works; the bibliography in a collection of essays presented to him on the occasion of his official retirement from his professorial chair at Nijmegen contained 391 entries up to December 1982. However, a list of those books which are readily available in English will form a useful point of reference and will give some idea of the range of Schillebeeckx's concerns. Because of the variable gaps between Dutch and English publications, the dates of both editions are given.[11]

Christ the Sacrament (1959, ET 1963) is an interpretation of the sacraments, and particularly the eucharist, in existentialist terms, as being an encounter with God.

Mary, Mother of the Redemption (1955, ET 1964) is a study of the church's beliefs about Mary as a means of deepening Christian spiritual life and devotion.

Marriage: Human Reality and Saving Mystery (1963, ET 1965) is a study of marriage in the Old and New Testaments and the history of the church in what was planned to be a two-volume work presenting a systematic theology of marriage. The second volume, meant to provide a synthesis of the historical evidence, never appeared.

Revelation and Theology (1964, ET 1967) is a collection of articles discussing the unity of scripture, tradition, theology and the faith of the ordinary contemporary believer as aspects of 'a dialogue between the living God and man'.

The Eucharist (1967, ET 1968) is an analysis and reinterpretation of the doctrine of transsubstantiation, first exploring the concerns of the Fathers who defined the doctrine at the Council of Trent and then developing a modern interpretation along the lines of *Christ the Sacrament*.

God and Man (1965, ET 1969) is a collection of articles particularly concerned with the problems of belief in God as they emerged in the 1960s, focussing on the growth of unbelief in a scientific age and the tendency of Christianity to undergo secularization, with a long discussion of the issues raised by John Robinson's *Honest to God*.

God the Future of Man (ET 1969, there was no Dutch edition) is a collection of articles largely given on a lecture tour in the United States two years previously, again mainly dealing with the question of secularization, but also touching on hermeneutics and politics.

World and Church (1965, ET 1971) is a collection of articles above all about the relationship between Christianity and humanism, seeing a positive relationship between the two.

The Mission of the Church (1968, ET 1973) is concerned with the reformation of the church, not least at the Second Vatican Council, and the differing roles played within it by clergy, laity and religious.

The Understanding of Faith (1972, ET 1974) contains articles largely on hermeneutics and critical theory as represented by Jürgen Habermas and the Frankfurt School.

Jesus: An Experiment in Christology (1974, ET 1979) is the first volume of Schillebeeckx's monumental investigation into the person

of Jesus and the way in which his life and death caused his followers
to believe that salvation was to be found in him.

Christ: The Christian Experience in the Modern World (1977, ET
1980; the original Dutch title was quite different: a translation would
be *Righteousness and Love; Grace and Liberation*) is the sequel to
Jesus, shifting its focus to the different ways in which the early
church responded to him with a view to seeing what our response
should be to him today.

Interim Report on the Books Jesus *and* Christ (1979, ET 1980), as
its title suggests, takes up a number of questions on which Schillebeeckx felt that he had not expressed himself sufficiently clearly or
on which he had been misunderstood.

Ministry: A Case for Change (1980, ET 1981) traces the development of the theology and form of the ministry from the New
Testament up to modern times, showing that 'modern' Roman
Catholic official views of the priesthood distort it as a ministry and
that the only way forward is radical change.

God among Us: The Gospel Proclaimed (1982, ET 1983) is a
collection of sermons and articles on spirituality, concluding with
the speech given by Schillebeeckx on his acceptance of the Erasmus
prize in 1982.

In addition to these books numerous articles have been translated
into English, many of them to be found in the issues of the journal
Concilium, with which Schillebeeckx is closely connected; others
have appeared in thematic collections of articles by various authors
which are often no longer easily accessible.

Bringing some order into this vast amount of writing is a bibliographer's nightmare, and the differences, often considerable, between the date of Dutch publication and that of English publication,
make a historical sequence more difficult to construct. In addition,
the thematic collections of articles sometimes contain material
spanning a wide period of time, thus making the actual date of
publication of the collection irrelevant. For example, the earliest
material in *Revelation and Theology* (1967) is dated 1945, and the
earliest material in *World and Church* (1971) is dated 1949, in each
case stemming from a very different world. Moreover the volumes
of collected articles in English, while translated from similar collections published first in Holland, do not exactly correspond with the
original.

However, once noted, these details need not concern us further here. Failure to take account of them could lead to misunderstandings, but it is in fact possible to trace the main themes of Schillebeeckx's thought without too much source analysis. That is because, especially in an introductory account of this kind, his most recent books are the most important. Although the division is not quite as simple as that, we may certainly see *Jesus* as a watershed. The distinction between Schillebeeckx the Catholic theologian of the church and Schillebeeckx the theologian of the world and the kingdom of God, which brings him into conflict with the church, as indicated at the beginning of this chapter, is a real one, and there is no doubt that for our time the latter concern is incomparably more interesting and, of course, more relevant. Those who have not progressed as far as he has (and every reader is likely to find Schillebeeckx ahead in one way or another) will still discover much of value and importance in the earlier works listed above and not referred to again; here, however, on the whole we shall essentially be concerned with *Jesus* and its successors in connection with a variety of questions.

Having followed the course of Schillebeeckx's life, so that we can see the background against which his writing is to be set, we shall be looking more closely at three groups of works represented by what to all intents and purposes are full-scale books: sacramental theology (*Christ the Sacrament* and *The Eucharist*); the meaning of Jesus (*Jesus*, and *Interim Report*); and the doctrine of ministry (*Ministry*). The first two books are the ones which antedate *Jesus*; for reasons which will be explained in due course, they form a good starting point. Alongside these investigations of books we shall look more thematically at issues which have particularly engaged Schillebeeckx: the whole question of salvation from God in Christ (discussed in *Christ* and elsewhere), spirituality (and especially Dominican spirituality), political theology and hermeneutics, before coming to a provisional assessment.

Because this is a portrait of a man who seems most to come alive when he is talking theology, and whose theology is his life, most of the pages which follow will be devoted to Schillebeeckx's books. Although he has given various interviews about his past, he is extremely sparing of personal anecdote: in the end he is a very private person. But that does not mean that his theology is impersonal; on the contrary, it is one of the most distinctively personal

contributions to modern theological thinking. If we are to appreciate
what he says, however, we need to spend more time than with other
writers on reflecting how best to read him. For here is more than at
times a bibliographer's nightmare; as may already be evident, these
are no ordinary books, and do not always follow the patterns with
which we may be familiar; an examination of the way in which the
author goes about his work may therefore in the long run save us a
good deal of puzzlement and help us to see more clearly what might
otherwise be extremely obscure.

First and foremost, when it comes to theology, Schillebeeckx is
all of a piece. Verbatim transcripts of interviews with journalists
prove to correspond word for word with passages published in his
books; chapters of full-scale works appear elsewhere as sermons or
articles; on some helpful occasions the substance of a whole volume
may be condensed into an article of a dozen or so pages, as happens,
for example, in the case of *Christ the Sacrament*.[12] These succinct
accounts of particular topics sometimes need to be supplemented
with larger-scale accounts if they are to become comprehensible; at
other times, as familiarity with his work grows, they provide
convenient guides to his more extended treatments. The interviews
may not always represent Schillebeeckx as he would like to present
himself, but particularly when the interviewer is aggressive and tries
to drive him into a corner they do have the advantage of making him
be precise – and he is too much of an old hand to find himself up
against the ropes!

Secondly, when reading Schillebeeckx you must imagine him
speaking. In a memorable passage Fr Ted Schoof, his assistant for
more than ten years, pictures him lecturing at Nijmegen: very fast,
with great emphasis, suggesting that virtually every sentence is of
vital importance. Most of the students scribble away as though
possessed, afraid of losing the thread, but never having time to
pause to see whether they in fact have hold of it. He always treats
them as equals, and always overestimates their capacity because he
measures it by his own. When this form of communication is
transferred to the printed page it leads to all kinds of emphases,
including a liberal use of italics.[13] Even when Schillebeeckx sets out
to write for a non-theological audience, as in *Jesus* or *Christ*, we
have to imagine ourselves in a lecture room with him at his desk in

front of us, except that we have the leisure to go back again and again over his words, with no fear of losing them.

Inevitably, this approach also has its negative side. For there is no doubt that for Schillebeeckx literary coherence and structure are a major problem. The list of his 'books' translated into English given above immediately reveals that the majority of the works are not books at all but fairly loose collections of articles. (Because publishers do not like collections of articles, in some cases this fact is fairly heavily disguised, so that a certain amount of detective work is needed in order to discover the true state of affairs.) However, that does not mean that one can go on to work with an absolute distinction between the two genres. Even if one leaves aside all the collections of articles and concentrates on the real books, it is clear that they have not been written like other literary works and are in constant danger of falling apart at the seams. The article, sermon or address is really the medium which Schillebeeckx finds most congenial, not least because in his busy life something else is always pressing, but as the topics which he tackles are usually far too big for such a small-scale form the time inevitably comes when he is forced to work on a larger canvas, and that is where his problems begin.

Christ, the sequel to *Jesus*, is a good example of what are often at first sight the bewildering characteristics and structural weaknesses of a big Schillebeeckx work. After two pages of prologue, largely in the form of a biblical meditation on Moses, and a further six and a half pages connecting the book with its predecessor, Schillebeeckx embarks on a masterly analysis of the nature of experience in the light of modern philosophy. Fifty pages later we are suddenly thrown into an enormous and fairly technical survey of the theology of the experience of grace in Old and New Testaments, a development which makes more sense when we remember the original Dutch title (see above). This analysis, beginning quite innocently with an examination of terminological usage, in fact turns into an account of the theologies of the New Testament writings apart from the first three Gospels and occupies some 450 pages. Because Schillebeeckx rightly holds that we cannot understand the experiences reflected in the New Testament in isolation from the world of the time, the next section considers various cultural and political aspects of that world which manage to lead up to a study of Christian responsibility for antisemitism and the claims of Israel to a land of its own. An attempt at a synthesis now follows, seeking to identify structural elements that will be included in any contemporary reinterpretation in which the gospel might be preserved while at the same time speaking to a different age. After only twenty-five pages of this (a lack of proportion in the different sections of a book is another Schillebeeckx characteristic), the scene changes completely and we look, first, at an account of mankind's preoccupation with utopias, hopes for the return of paradises past or for the creation of paradises to come, followed, secondly, by a survey of ideas of suffering in all the major religions of the world up to and including the Enlightenment and Marxism. This is followed by a discussion of the question 'What is man?', immediately succeeded by a consideration of the question 'What is history?' After that we come to what promises to be the conclusion, an account of the nature of 'Salvation from God, experienced through man and the world'. However, the author realizes that this marathon course, which has already taken him more than 800 pages, and is the originally unplanned sequel to an earlier study of almost the same length, cannot yet be concluded because there are relevant factors of which he has not yet taken account. So, as we saw earlier, he brings it to an end with liturgical material of various kinds and promises another, third, volume as a conclusion.

When we realize that *Jesus* ended in a similarly haphazard way, necessitating the insertion at the last minute of an unexpected piece of systematic theology which has puzzled readers since and the presence of which the author felt called to explain at some length later, it is evident that here we have come up against a basic characteristic of Schillebeeckx's *modus operandi*. If, therefore, we can make sense of what at first sight seems to be an almost over-ambitious treatment of a huge amount of often disparate material, we shall be well on the way towards understanding the way in which he thinks and will be able to join him in his explorations with more profit. And in fact we *can* make good sense of it all. If in due course you compare this somewhat disparaging account with the thematic treatment of 'Salvation from God' in Chapter 6 below, you will be more aware of the inner logic which holds this material together, even when the outward form threatens to pull it apart.

There is no question that Schillebeeckx has one of the best and acutest minds of all twentieth-century theologians, and arguably the best grounding in theological thought over the whole range of Christian tradition, not to mention modern philosophy. This is evident most of all where he ventures to write, as he does in, say *Jesus*, on completely new subject-matter after what is by any academic standards a relatively short space of time. Time and again in the pages of that book one comes across shrewd judgments, expressed succinctly, which would not disgrace a professional New Testament scholar arriving at the end of a detailed investigation. How many of the countless books on the quest for the historical Jesus, for example, ever came up with anything as good as this?

> What happens when the historical method is systematically applied in assessing Jesus is, after all, a qualitative change imposed upon the ordinary spontaneous apprehension or recollection of a person from the past. And however well supported historically this scientifically created image may be, the first disciples of Jesus were never confronted with this likeness – even though it be wholly relevant to the Jesus who was then living and whom the churches now acknowledge as the Christ.[14]

A more extended instance can be found in *The Eucharist*, the study in which he reinterprets for modern times the traditional doctrine of transsubstantiation. This is how he begins his investigation:

> We know from the whole history of theology that it is always dangerous simply to repeat a formulation of faith which was made in a different climate of thought in the past and that if we do so it is hardly possible to speak of a *living* affirmation of faith. According to the *Constitution on Revelation*, it is impossible to grasp the real biblical meaning of scripture without a knowledge of the various literary genres and the distinctive forms of thought of the writers of the Old and New Testaments. What theologians openly apply to Scripture, which is inspired, they must just as openly venture to apply to Conciliar statements. What is remarkable, however, is that some Christians show more reverence for these statements than they do for the Bible. Nevertheless we must persevere in putting this method into practice if we are to be faithful to God's revealing word.[15]

Here, as succinctly and clearly as one could wish, is an account of the programme of 'doctrinal criticism', the concern to subject the

doctrines and doctrinal texts of the church, including the doctrine of
the incarnation and the creeds, to the same kind of historical
criticism as had already been applied for a century. And remarkably,
it is all but contemporaneous with the pioneering statement of aims
made by George Woods in England, later to be taken up to
considerable effect by Maurice Wiles.[16]

The same gift can also be noted in his treatments of historical
figures and developments in the past (his account of Albertus
Magnus in Chapter 7 below is a good example). His achievement in
this connection has been likened, in a brilliant comparison, to the
work of musicians like Nicholas Harnoncourt or Christopher Hog-
wood in blowing away the dust from earlier music and allowing us to
hear, understand and enjoy it in quite a new way; similarly, Schillebeeckx brings the past alive by taking us into its *world* – and his
achievement here (and that of those like Marie-Dominique Chenu,
who inspired him) is evident if one compares his work with the dry
interpretation of theological *texts* which was so characteristic of
earlier generations of Catholic theology.

Many of Schillebeeckx's brilliant judgments – and the depth and
quality of them can often be missed because, as in so much of the
rest of his work, one should really know and have read as much as
he has to savour them to the full – are often thrown out in passing,
and are incidental to the detail of the argument. And as we have
seen, the course of that argument is often difficult to follow and calls
for all our attention. There are identifiable reasons for this.

First of all, Schillebeeckx can set out without knowing where he
is going to end up. He makes this quite clear himself in a personal
statement in his *Interim Report*, in which he takes up points in his
Jesus and *Christ* on which he feels that he has been either misunderstood or misrepresented. A Belgian New Testament scholar had
argued that his biblical interpretation was too much governed by the
theological systematization which was to come later, and presupposed the views for which Schillebeeckx was to argue. Schillebeeckx
retorted: 'he requires of an exegete that he should embark on his
quest without knowing exactly where he will end up; in fact, I
remarked (in the *Jesus* book) that I was embarking on an exegetical
search without knowing in advance where this would take me,
precisely what he requires of proper exegesis! . . . I could not in fact
work towards a christology which was already presupposed, because

this only becomes clear at the end of the study and then only rather vaguely: the book still bears traces of this. Once the result became clear, however, when I worked over the book for the last time I made insertions into the earlier sections which would lead up to the final conclusion, so as to give the book a better construction.'[17]

Add to that the fact that Schillebeeckx is clearly extremely loathe ever to scrap or even leave aside anything that he has written – he has preserved all the notes he has made on his reading, from his earliest days – and the precise nature of his works and the problems that they present becomes abundantly clear. Putting things in an over-simple way for the sake of clarity, his process of working would seem to be something like this.

By virtue of his wide reading and ability to see a question from many different perspectives, when he tackles a subject, Schillebeeckx will want to get to the heart of it by taking into account not only its nucleus, but also all the other issues which come up in connection with it. Because these issues may take him into realms far removed from his main concern, a large-scale book is likely to turn into a series of discussions each clustering round a different focal point, with his readers left to join the focal points themselves and make sense of their conjunction. They are left, in other words, to use the evidence presented to them, not always in the arrangement that they would expect, in order to reconstruct the pattern of Schillebeeckx's thought and to share his insights and moments of illumination with him. The final book, even if things worked out well, would therefore, by virtue of its very ground plan, present difficulties.

But things do not always turn out well. Because sometimes he sets out not knowing where his investigations are going to take him, Schillebeeckx can find himself going in an unplanned direction, or even discover that his investigations do not lead him to any coherent and firm conclusion (this is particularly evident in the case of the large body of exegetical material at the heart of *Christ*). That loosens the structure at times almost to breaking point. As we have seen, a book which one might have thought would come to a conclusion all but peters out, leaving it 'to be continued in our next' (it would be very easy to see the sequence begun by *Jesus* and *Christ* ending only as a result of human mortality!). At times the development of Schillebeeckx's own thought makes the earlier stages of planned large-scale works incomplete, so that they are abandoned as torsos (this is evident from his first work on the sacraments, *De sacramentele heilseconomie*, only half written and never translated, and his book on marriage).

Nor do the complications end there. Again as Schillebeeckx points out in his *Interim Report*, once a text is on a printed page it takes on a life of its own; it has become an independent objective entity apart from its author. What he has written, he has written. But as long as the author is alive he is accessible for questions on that text which may lead to other writings,[18] or looking at it in cold print he may feel that it fails to say all that he intended, so that he has to add to it or qualify it in various ways, particularly if, like Schillebeeckx, he is quite open to criticism and very ready to accept it and act upon it. Thus a second generation of writings grows up around the original work, rather like a commentary on it, and woe betide any serious contributor to the discussion who has not grasped them as well as the basic text. As we shall see,[19] this *caveat* applies to his book on *Ministry* as well as to *Jesus* and *Christ*.

Perhaps the best word for describing Schillebeeckx's method, then, is cumulative: perspective is added to perspective until we have considered the subject from every possible angle. 'Cumulative' is also the best word to describe the construction of his writings on a smaller scale: the paragraph, the section or the chapter. Where another author might make a number of drafts, tear several of them up, and attempt to distil what he wanted to say into a sequence of well-polished sentences, Schillebeeckx goes on adding one sentence to another, one phrase to another and even one word to another. Attention has been drawn more than once to his tendency to use pairs of words where one would do: 'other alternatives', 'apparently seems', 'exclusive monopoly', 'affirmatively endorse', and so on. (A tendency which proves infectious for those who steep themselves in his writing, as was evident from the first draft of this book.) Cumulative near-tautology is a Schillebeeckx characteristic which derives in part from his lecturing – one can see the oratorical effect – and in part from his painstaking concern to express precisely what he seeks to convey. If one statement does not quite say what he means, he may add a second to supplement it which in part may overlap the first, until all the significance of what he wants to draw out has been extracted. Consequently his books are also peppered with phrases like 'in other words', 'at the same time', 'to put it another way', 'it follows immediately from this' and so on. That is partly why the books – and indeed some of Schillebeeckx's articles – are so long.[20]

I have come to the conclusion that Schillebeeckx's works are perhaps best described in musical terms: here is the extended language and loose structure of nineteenth-century romanticism rather than the ordered regularity of classical sonata form. And having decided that quite independently, I discovered that Schillebeeckx's long-time assistant had in fact compared him with Anton Bruckner (another person who was very ready to listen to suggestions for altering his works).

> Schillebeeckx shares Bruckner's splendid breadth of vision, his intensity and his uncomplicated 'southern' attitude. Many of his writings too have the 'resounding' quality of Bruckner's music and full justice can often only be done to the repetitions, full of subtle changes of emphasis, that they contain, when they are rendered oratorically.[21]

That is true, even if – as we have seen – Schillebeeckx is hardly Bruckner's equal when it comes to structure. In the face of this tendency towards what seems like a lack of cohesion, one habit of Schillebeeckx's helps to keep his work together and enables the reader to find his bearings. A variety of favourite phrases and terms keep recurring as the focal point of a cluster of thought. At first sight one may well pass them by because they are not always obvious. They can be as unobtrusive as 'creation faith (or belief in creation)' or 'salvation from God in Jesus', building up through longer phrases like 'God's concern as man's concern' or 'God's glory is man's happiness', to quite extended statements like 'salvation from God through the mediation of Jesus as the eschatological prophet of the coming kingdom of God', which recurs regularly in the *Jesus* book. To keep the musical metaphor, these terms and phrases serve as themes which can be orchestrated and developed in a variety of ways. Sometimes Schillebeeckx engages as it were in musicological analysis and shows us what the elements in their structure are which make them so versatile; at other times he simply uses them in larger structures, introducing new contexts, new harmonies, new resonance, while never allowing us to forget that we have heard the themes before and can bring our own associations from elsewhere to them. Perhaps it is this way of working that gives his theology not just an intellectual but also an emotional appeal, so amply attested by the existence of the many unexpected and untrained readers among his audience.

And if we then look more closely, we may begin to note the way in which he uses a variety of words – more than can in fact be rendered into English, and some of them compounds with multiple hyphens, to indicate that in his own mind at any rate, all the different elements which so far have seemed constantly to be in danger of falling apart are in fact held together in a unity of vision. The way in which he can tell an anxious publisher that his new work (likely to run to six or seven hundred pages) is 'finished, and all that remains is to write it', words which he has used on more than one occasion,[22] confirms that he envisages projects of enormous magnitude well before actually setting out to realize them on paper. Just how much this is the case can be seen from a work of more manageable size than *Jesus* or *Christ*, namely *Ministry*, in which the detailed investigation of the historical development of ministry and the conclusions which are drawn from this investigation for the pattern that the church should adopt for its ministry in the twentieth century so flow into each other that the whole account is dominated by a sense of inevitability – which raises other problems that we shall be considering later.[23]

Some of this analysis may not have seemed particularly complimentary, and indeed at times may have been almost damning. In pointing towards a possible way into Schillebeeckx's works I have also had to indicate problems and weaknesses. But had these problems been as serious as all that, I could have found better things to do than to spend a considerable amount of time reading him and translating him, not to mention writing this book. The fact of the matter is – to revert to music for a last time – that it is possible to compose works with impeccable structure and great complexity which are nevertheless not engaging enough to make one want to explore all their many facets: when one listens to them they are just plain academic and dull. Whatever else – and we have looked at that qualification – Schillebeeckx has some marvellous tunes, and at his best he uses them as all the best composers do, not only to delight the mind by the ideas behind them but also to warm the heart and make the body respond. At his best he achieves something the possibility of which he investigated in his student days: transcending mere thinking in terms of rational concepts to provide a glimpse of the glory of God, a glory which, however, in his view can never be seen unless it is set off against the history of human suffering and the wretchedness of man that cries out for our efforts towards liberation and relief and for God's new creation.

So much by way of introduction. It is now time to follow Schillebeeckx on some of his explorations. But before we do that we need to discover something more about the man himself and the course of his life.

2

Life

Those who know something of the way in which Edward Schille-beeckx lives and works never cease to be amazed at the sheer amount of what he manages to achieve. The length of his two major books (the English translation of *Jesus* runs to 786pp. and that of *Christ* to 926pp.) makes them daunting enough to read, let alone to have written, and they in fact represent only a small proportion of all his published writings, besides the courses of lectures which he has given during his teaching career. If one then looks at the extensive footnotes and bibliographies, referring not just to modern works in many languages but to the whole range of classical Christian writings, from the Bible and the early Fathers onwards, and an overwhelming amount of modern philosophical writing, his achieve-ment verges on the incredible. For all his amazing capacity to read and assimilate books at a great speed while taking notes on them, to accomplish this, for many years he made a habit of beginning to work in the evening, after supper, and continuing through to the small hours, then being woken in the morning by his alarm clock to carry on with his other responsibilities. And those have been many, since after all, for the last twenty-five years he has been a university professor as well as a Dominican, with a long-standing inability to say 'no' which has led him to accept a wide range of speaking engagements all over the Netherlands, not to mention editorial responsibilities in connection with various journals, and has been a much sought-after figure for newspaper, radio and television interviews.

And that is only part of the story. Being an international celebrity, whether he wants that or not, Schillebeeckx is much in demand for lectures and conferences round the world, and does a good deal of travelling. He travels regularly to the United States for marathon visits: one year he gave no fewer than forty-two lectures in a two-month tour.

This vitality he ascribes not least to the example and inherited characteristics of his father, Constant Johannes Schillebeeckx, who according to Edward was incapable of doing nothing, could not bring himself to retire until he was eighty-two, lived to be ninety-five, and was obviously a major influence on Edward's life. All his life Edward's father proved a firm support. While the rest of the family did not really understand Edward's books, and particularly after Vatican II came to see him as something of a renegade, his father read them all for as long as he was physically able, even including dictionary articles. He understood what he read and was behind it to the point of making a memorable comment. When the soundness of Edward's writings was investigated for the first time, in 1968, his father was asked whether he wasn't horrified that his son should be under investigation by the Pope. 'I don't know the Pope,' he replied, 'but I do know our Edward and I trust him.' Everything that Edward says about his father makes it clear that Constant Johannes was his great inspiration: 'an Old Testament patriarch in the best sense of the phrase'.

What can be gleaned about Edward Schillebeeckx's early years, before his theological training began, is important. As he himself has remarked, many studies of theologians begin with their first theological teachers, whereas by that stage much will already have happened that is decisive for their later development. That is certainly so in his case.

Edward Cornelis Florentius Alfons Schillebeeckx was born on 12 November 1914, in Antwerp, in Belgium.[1] His parents originally came from Geel, half-way and slightly to the south between Antwerp and Eindhoven in Holland, and had settled at Kortenberg, a small town some twelve miles east of Brussels, in the direction of Louvain. He was the sixth of fourteen children, nine boys and five girls. His father was a chartered accountant who often found himself acting as receiver for bankrupt companies, which could mean investigating the possibility of fraud. He was well-to-do, fond of parties and very much a family man. Both he and his wife, Johanna Petronella (née Calis), clearly had high standards, but were understanding and approachable, giving each of their children a sense of individuality and in effect leaving them to bring one another up. The family was a very close one, not least because its mere size and Constant Johannes' profession set them somewhat apart. They still come together for a reunion twice a year. They were also good Catholics, though Constant Johannes was determinedly anti-clerical. When Edward came home for the first time after his ordination to the priesthood his mother had the temerity to suggest that he should now say grace at dinner. Constant Johannes thereupon banged the table and asserted, 'In this house I'm the priest.' There were a great many house prayers, and the family went to mass every day at 6.30 in the morning.

This Catholic family atmosphere comes through very clearly in Edward's earliest memories. They are connected with the family crib, still preserved, which would stand in a corner of the living room on a table, with large paper figures: a caravan of camels, the three kings and the crib with the Christ child. When the children were young, Constant Johannes would use the figures to explain the Christmas stories. Pointing to the baby in the crib, he would say, 'That child is God'. At that time Edward would have been about four or five years old. In 1920, at the age of six, he went to the primary school in Kortenberg; because of the war he had no kindergarten schooling. It was about then that he also began to serve at mass, and that too made an impression on him; it was different from ordinary life and aroused deep feelings. Although he was rather more serious and less talkative than his brothers and sisters, he did not stand out as being particularly pious. But then he was not to be the only priest from a remarkable family, the members of which were all intellectual and as well as priests included a doctor, three engineers and two accountants.

Family discipline was a combination of strictness and freedom. The children were allowed to go out as they wanted provided that they were back at the agreed time. There was a distinctive way of dealing with those who had misbehaved. The parents had a custom of making the sign of the cross on the children's foreheads before they went to sleep; Constant Johannes (but never his wife) omitted to do this if anyone had been bad. That, Edward remarked, settled things without further ado; forgiveness was represented by the restoration of the sign of the cross the next day.

This arrangement had clearly been worked out between the

parents, who seem to have complemented one another well. Although Constant Johannes was the more intellectual, at the same time he was more emotional than his wife; on the occasion of their diamond wedding Edward said that for all his intellectual gifts, his father was the heart of the family, while his mother provided the common sense.

The boys of the family went to the Jesuit school at Turnhout, not far from their parents' old home; Edward moved there in 1926. Soon after he arrived, he found that instead of proceeding through the senior school he had to go back and repeat the last two years of the junior school course, largely because of language problems. (Teaching at the Jesuit school was in French whereas his education at Kortenberg had been in Flemish.) This demotion is clearly one reason, as he himself acknowledges, why he has worked so hard all through his life. Turnhout was the strictest of the Jesuit colleges: no contact with the outside world and hard discipline. Edward felt that he was exiled from his family. He found it a prison, and never really accepted it: it was 'all rules and duty'. The teaching was of a very high standard, but extremely utilitarian: for example, it led to great competence in Latin and Greek but too little appreciation of their beauties. Once he had arrived in the senior school he was always top of the class; characteristically, he still has all the notes on his reading from that time.

Three teachers from this period stand out in his mind. First was Fr Seeldraaijers, one of the pioneers of the Flemish movement. He taught Greek and Latin and not only gave Edward a thorough grounding in them – he was very brilliant and could even improvise in Greek – but also helped him to think. Unlike most of his colleagues, he went beyond the mere subject-matter of his teaching and discussed wider issues. As a result of this approach he aroused Edward's interest in the East. Edward became fascinated by the differences between Hinduism, Buddhism, Islam and Christianity and wanted to explore them further in British India. (An older brother had gone out as a Jesuit and was to spend his life there.) Letters home from this period show his expectations quite clearly; he even thought of cycling to India! However, missionary work was not his concern; his interest was more in differences in patterns of thought between religions: he detected a version of the Trinity in

Hinduism. Fr Seeldraaijers also had difficulties with his Order, a fact which intrigued Edward: another portent for the future.

A Fr Notebaert interested him in social, economic and political problems, and in philosophy – interests which were to remain with him all his life. However, in this connection Fr de Witte proved even more important. He was a social worker, and through him, the theory of social questions was extended to actual practice. At that time those being taught at the Jesuit school were something of an elite, and while heavy demands were laid on them in other directions, they were relieved of a number of more menial chores. About twenty less privileged local boys of twelve or thirteen years of age were brought in off the streets to make beds, serve at table and so on for a small wage. Fr de Witte thought that this kind of exploitation was not right and saw that the boys were also given lessons. A newspaper was also produced for them and Edward was involved in the writing of it.

However, Edward did not accept all Fr de Witte's views. In particular he disagreed with him over principles and disciplinary matters. Edward was told off for talking with one of his fellow students at a time when he should have been working in his room on his own. It was explained to him that this was forbidden on principle. 'I don't care for principles,' Edward retorted, 'he needed me.' Inevitably, Edward's time with the Jesuits was not to last. The teaching and the atmosphere were too dull and formal, and the discipline too rigid. The year before the pupils' final year at the school, it was the practice to take the whole class to a retreat house where they would be addressed by well-known preachers and encouraged to spend the rest of their lives in the Order. Successful though this process of indoctrination might have been with others, with Edward it had the opposite effect. Although by the time he left Turnhout the idea of India had faded, he still felt the need for a pattern of life which offered rather more individual freedom than that of the Jesuits and was less strictly ascetic.

Towards the end of his schooling, Edward had begun to read systematically the lives of St Ignatius Loyola, St Dominic, St Francis and St Benedict. As a result of this he resolved to be a Dominican. Why he made this choice is something that he still cannot explain; it was hardly, he says, a cerebral decision. Certainly, however, it was not as a result of any personal contact: he had never met a

Dominican. The 'gentle and fascinating personality' of Dominic made an emotional appeal, while on the intellectual side he discovered that Dominic had inspiration and cared little for rules. Figures from the later history of the Order whom we shall meet later, like Albertus Magnus, Thomas Aquinas and Père Lacordaire,[2] also made their mark. All in all, Edward saw in the Order a tension between two poles, those of religion and of life in the world, an insight which was another pointer towards the future. When he told his plans to his father, he received a characteristic response: 'Edward, I hope that it's not a sudden whim and that you've thought hard about it. But as far as I'm concerned, do what you want.'

Edward was now nineteen, and since he did not know any Dominicans, he had to set out in search of them. Because of the strict Jesuit discipline, this involved a secret correspondence. He discovered that he would have to serve his novitiate in Ghent, and got in touch with the Prior of the Dominican community there, Fr Matthijs, who was also Professor of Metaphysics and Theology in the University of Ghent. The Prior responded by inviting him over for a week in the summer vacation, enclosing with his invitation a picture depicting a detail from a Fra Angelico fresco in which St Dominic is embracing St Francis. The warmth and harmony which the picture conveyed made a deep impression. Among the Jesuits, personal friendships had been forbidden and emotions repressed, but a gesture by an unknown Dominican had suddenly opened up quite a different world. In the event, coming to Ghent was like coming home.

As at home, a good deal was asked of him; but he was treated as an equal, and the discipline was administered with love. The teaching, too, was a revelation: in contrast to the rather austere theological catechetics of Turnhout. He describes the year's novitiate, beginning in September 1934, as a time of much praying, choral offices and meditation, along with lecture courses about the monastic life. In his free time he read the great mystics: Rusbroeck, St Teresa of Avila, St Catherine of Siena, St John of the Cross, Meister Eckhardt and Henricus Suso. (In fact he took Henricus Suso as his Dominican name and was known by it virtually until he moved to Nijmegen; it was then dropped, partly because the university there used civil rather than religious names.) However, it was his father rather than any mystic who was to provide him with the most educative experience of the novitiate. Edward had written home about the deep impression made on him by the Dominican night office, from 3 a.m. to 4 a.m., while 'people outside' were sleeping. His father replied in a down-to-earth way. 'My boy, your mother and I have to get up three or four times a night [they had just had their fourteenth child] to calm a crying baby, and that is less romantic than your night office. Think about it: religion is not an emotional state but an attitude of service.' Edward was never, he said, so ashamed as when he read and reread this letter. Forty years later he was to say that its words were still engraved on his heart, that they had influenced his theological thinking and made him antipathetic to religious ideology.

He then moved on to Louvain for three years' philosophy. Fr Perquin, the Prior there, was also President of the Social Schools in Louvain and his influence heightened Edward's practical social concerns. Edward describes these three years as the best of his life. There he came particularly under the influence of Fr de Petter, the Dominican philosopher, who was spiritual director of the young Dominicans as well as being senior Professor of Philosophy in the University of Ghent. De Petter's interests were very close to those of Edward's at the time, and Edward describes him as *the* great background to his education. De Petter allowed and encouraged Edward to read Kant, Hegel and Freud, although they were officially banned; his own approach was phenomenological, and both socio-logy and psychology played a major role in his understanding of human nature. De Petter also taught Edward something else: the absolute priority of grace over all human effort. At that time Edward learnt, he has said, that God is to be trusted, so that he has never been worried about himself or about anything else. Not least, de Petter introduced Edward to the German theologian Karl Adam, whose works *The Nature of Catholicism* (1928) and *Christ our Brother* (1934) enjoyed a particular vogue at that time. The way in which Adam went back beyond scholasticism to Augustine and the Church Fathers differentiated him from other Catholic writers of the period and appealed to Edward. Moreover, at a time when Catholics and Protestants tended to go their separate ways and much Catholic biblical interpretation was narrowly traditionalist, Adam showed an appreciation of biblical criticism; he also wrote about the psychology of Jesus. This led Edward towards an overriding interest in experience, a factor which had almost been completely neglected in post-Tridentine theology. De Petter encouraged him in this direction by asking him to produce a study of the way in which conceptuality could be transcended. This led him to explore the nature of intuition, the experience of the world and with it the experience of meaning. Again, this was to be an important pointer to his future concerns, though what he wrote at that time was a far cry from the masterly discussion of experience which opens *Christ*.

In the summer of 1938, Edward had to do his compulsory military service, since even clergy were conscripted. However, they did have the privilege of free time for theological reading. Edward was posted to Leopoldsburg, midway between Louvain and Eindhoven, which was the base for clergy conscripts. It was there that he met pastors from non-Catholic churches, conversation with whom broadened his horizons further. He was fortunate in that his chaplain, Fr Van der Elst, managed to have him exempted from everything but first aid, so that he could simply press on with his studies; he even rented a private room in which to study. He would spend days on end reading Kant; he was also introduced to Heidegger, Husserl and Merleau-Ponty, and the seeds were sown for his later interest in Marxism.

After his year's military service he returned to Louvain to continue his studies, but with the outbreak of war in September 1939 he was called up again, a month later, in the general mobilization. As a soldier he saw virtually nothing of the war, being moved around on various postings until hostilities began in May 1940, and then 'sitting in a village for a couple of weeks or so, after which we all went home' – in his case, back to his studies at Louvain.

His three years' philosophy completed, he now embarked on a course of three years' theology. In comparison with philosophy he found this old-fashioned. The only exception among his teachers was a Fr Martin, a mediaeval historian who approached Thomas Aquinas historically rather than in a literal fashion, text by text, like the other professors. As always, he acquired the reputation of being a hard worker, said constantly to be writing and reading.

In addition to academic work he was also involved in the Dominican student magazine, *The Beehive*, and even wrote an entire issue, of mammoth size, single-handed. This was in his last year of

theology, 1942-43, during which a speech by Karl Adam, 'Christianity in the New Order', had been circulated secretly among the
students. We have already seen the influence Adam was having;
Edward was particularly attracted by his treatment of nature and
supernature, but could not accept other aspects of the thought of
someone so positive towards National Socialism, so he produced a
300-page article in reply. This in fact was his first 'book'. Even at this
stage he planned to go on to write a book about Jesus, but it would
be a while before that plan bore fruit. Edward was ordained priest
in 1941; in that same year De Petter was dismissed by the Vatican
from his teaching post, and at the same time Fr Charlier and Fr
Chenu (whom we shall meet shortly) were also condemned. This
too made a deep impression on Edward: what he had *experienced* as
the truth had been condemned by Rome. However, he saw this as
experience in learning to take setbacks. He had never set great store
by becoming a priest, as he pointed out in the Dutch Dominican
journal *De Bazuin* on the occasion of the fortieth anniversary of his
ordination to the priesthood. It was the Dominican Order that had
attracted him and the priesthood was something which had as it were
happened in addition. He grew into it, and came to see religious life
as a pattern which gave the priesthood a special colouring of its own.

Because of his intellectual preoccupations, Edward acquired the
reputation of being somewhat stand-offish; those who did not know
him well could easily misread his apparent attitudes towards them.
Perhaps with some justification, because his single-mindedness
inevitably shaped his reactions. He clearly knew what he wanted
from his training: because of his discontent with speculative theology
he devoted his last two years' study to exegesis, and the thesis by
which he obtained his doctorate, in 1943, was on the concept of *sarx*
in Paul. This was immediately followed by an appointment as
lecturer in dogmatic theology at Louvain, and there he remained
until the end of the war.

Anyone reconstructing the outline of Edward Schillebeeckx's
career may be struck by the minor part played in it by the Second
World War. Had he been in Holland, with its large Jewish population
and political administration, things might have been different. As it
is, one must remember that he is a Belgian, and that in Belgium
circumstances were different. Under a military regime with a general
married to a Belgian wife, life was less unbearable, and while

Edward will not have been unaware of the traumas of Nazi tyranny, they made less of a direct impact.

After the war, he spent two years doing post-doctoral study in Paris. Officially he was at Le Saulchoir, the famous Dominican theological school just outside Paris, but he also went to lectures at the Sorbonne, where Etienne Gilson, the famous philosopher, and Eduard Dhorme, the great Old Testament scholar, were lecturing. He also learned a great deal from the patristic scholar Charles Puech, who taught him how to analyse texts. At Le Saulchoir, Edward first made the acquaintance of the doyen ecumenist Yves Congar, but the figure who towered above all others was Marie-Dominique Chenu, whom he has called the greatest theologian of the century. What struck Edward most about Chenu was his combination of historical analysis and reconstruction of church tradition with involvement in the world. It was the former approach which taught Edward the importance of going back to the sources; this developed his historical sense and contributed towards that mastery of documents from all periods of the church which is such an impressive feature of his writing and argumentation. The latter concern accorded very much with a trait in Edward that we have already noted.

Chenu inspired Edward not just through his writings, which in fact were not very extensive, but by the whole force of his personality. Edward saw him as a prophet whose vision of the future could provide hope for the present, a prophet who above all else represented freedom. Here, for Edward, was the embodiment of the Dominican ideal, concern before God for the world, rather than just for the church, and priority for the world's problems: Chenu began his theology from the 'signs of the times'. This attitude of course led to tension with the Vatican (as we have seen, Chenu's book about the theological approach he wanted to follow at Le Saulchoir had already been condemned in 1941). Chenu's *The Social Doctrine of the Church as Ideology*, published later, with its acute and inexorable analysis of the ideology underlying the papal social encyclicals of the past century, illustrates this emphasis well. A political theologian before 'political theology' became a common term, Chenu would talk of the church as 'a church of the poor and humble', 'the messianic community of the poor'.

Because Chenu was such an influence on Edward's life, it is worth quoting some of his own words about himself:

It might be thought that there are two Chenus. One is an old mediaevalist, not without a certain reputation, entirely absorbed in his reading of ancient texts, full of learning and attached to the early centuries of Christianity, a tradition to which he clings in the middle of the present century. Then there is the other Chenu, young, energetic, almost frivolous, caught up in the bustle of the modern world, very sensitive to its demands, quick to commit himself to the most critical problems of the world and the church and for some time now a controversial figure who is suspect in certain quarters. But this is not true – there is only one Chenu. The unity of theology is revealed in this paradoxical unity of two personalities and two commitments – the word of God in the world, where the Spirit even now still continues and realizes the meaning of Christ's incarnation in human thinking both individually and collectively.[2]

At Le Saulchoir, Edward also made the close acquaintance of Marxist and anti-Christian philosophers; Chenu introduced him personally to Albert Camus, with whom he had many discussions. He was struck by the inconsistency of Camus, 'a fascinating man', who could say 'I find Christianity abhorrent' and yet spend so much time at Le Saulchoir and have many Dominican friends. This was also the period of the attempt of a rapprochement between Catholics and Communists, and of the worker-priest movement, which again brought home to Edward that faith and piety were not enough. In his own words: 'Our bourgeois society is always concerned that piety should be kept within limits and should not be an inspiration towards action or a force in social and economic commitment.' From this point onwards it was no longer possible, if it ever had been, to do theology by going into a study and shutting the door.

In 1947 he was summoned back to Louvain to teach dogmatic theology. He had wanted to write his next thesis, required for him to become qualified as a teacher, on nature and supernature, religion and the world, but in Louvain he was expected to lecture on the sacraments; hence they became the subject of the thesis and his first real book. At this stage he was still involved in pastoral work as well. For eight years he was chaplain to the prison in Louvain, hearing confessions and celebrating the eucharist once a week: much of his work was in connection with people who had collaborated with the Germans during the war. Initially, along with other young priests there he would also go out each week to preach in country parishes. In addition, he was closely involved with students. He was their spiritual director, and also lectured on pastoral matters and gave liturgical training, for example on how to celebrate mass. As a result he found himself living in two worlds. On the one hand he was responsible, in fact, not only for lecturing on the sacraments, but for all the dogmatics teaching in the college, so that over a four-year period he would lecture on everything from creation to eschatology, a course which he covered two and a half times, thoroughly revising his material each time round. On the other, he was trying to work out a satisfactory relationship with the students, which would differ from the regime that had gone before, under his former teacher de Petter. Greatly influenced by his father's approach, Edward could never inflict punishment, and gave his students great latitude, which caused problems with the authorities; there was even an attempt to remove him from his post of Director of students. From this period comes a first attempt to characterize Dominican spirituality, which was eventually to be published in a revised form thirty years later.[3] Edward's social concerns continued. At that time the books of René Voillaume were extremely popular; Edward bought them for his students, who devoured them. Because of current interest in the worker-priest movement, he found himself discussing Voillaume's views and the movement, not uncritically, with the students, some of whom wanted to go in this direction. And again, after Paris, things could not be restricted to talk and reading. One controversial move in which he was involved was to take two coach-loads of students to the frontier with East Germany to visit a progressive pastor there who was working with refugees. Edward and the students helped the pastor to build a reception centre; they worked during the day and talked theology in the evenings. It was an experience which led him to attach great importance to small communities.

However, all the time at Louvain theology was gradually winning, and as his teaching and study continued, it took up an increasing amount of his time and so that it became clear that he would spend the rest of his life as an academic theologian. This followed inevitably from the professionalism with which he approached theology, never content with second-hand judgments but always going back to primary material. Moreover, even while he was in Louvain he was in constant demand in Holland by organizations and periodicals concerned for renewal within the church. It was this increasing public recognition together with his not inconsiderable achievements, along with an affinity to the pragmatic element in Dutch theology, which eventually brought him to live there permanently.

He was called to be Professor of Dogmatics and the History of Theology in the University of Nijmegen, and took up his post in January 1958. There he came to live at the Albertinum, the vast Dutch Dominican house, where he still shares the life of the Dutch Order. After Louvain, in some respects Nijmegen seemed to Edward to be very conservative, and he felt as though he were going back to the Middle Ages. Generally speaking, however, this move brought with it a new approach in his theological work. In part this arose from the new conditions there. In Nijmegen there were very few students there, barely forty of them, almost all priests. This meant, first, that his theological teaching could be at a high level and on subjects to a large extent of his own choosing; he did not have to teach courses which distracted him from his main interests. Secondly – at least in theory – he would have much more time for writing.[4]

However, things did not turn out quite like that. He felt so much at home in Holland that he would accept virtually any engagements which came his way. As a result, what should have been more time for study was taken up with travelling all over the place; being selective in his choice was not one of Edward's strong points. The contacts which he made in this way proved important for his subsequent theology and explain his stress on the importance of theology beginning from the level of the community. However, the pace which Edward set himself could not last, and in 1960 he had to take an enforced rest from overworking.

This was the time when the Second Vatican Council was first announced, and Edward was involved in the preparatory work from the start. At the end of 1960 he made an important contribution to a letter issued by the Dutch bishops, and as a result of his contribution was eventually invited to go to Rome. Not, however, as an official expert; this was probably because he came to be regarded as the 'author' of the Dutch bishops' letter, which was thought to be so influenced by 'new theology' that the Italian version of it was withdrawn by the censors.

Vatican II was particularly important for him because now, for the first time, he could meet and talk at length with the main creative theologians from outside Holland. People who had previously read one another's books could get to know one another personally, and that led to many new friendships. Edward also made the acquaintance of many of the bishops and saw how overburdened they were with their enormous pastoral problems. In fact his main work at the Council was giving lectures to very different groups of bishops, sometimes two hundred at a time, about what he found good or otherwise in the basic documents discussed at the Council. One problem there had proved to be that when the Council began, no papers had been published which provided any criticisms of the documents on which it was to focus. Edward's work of critical interpretation therefore played a vital role, and his contributions were translated and distributed in numbers of up to two thousand. Inevitably, such work got him into trouble and at one stage there had to be a public announcement that his lectures did not have the official approval of the Council. Less directly, through the advice he gave to Dutch bishops, much of his thinking found its way into the official sessions.

Looking back on Vatican II, Edward's criticisms typically took two opposed directions. On the one hand he was very conscious of how unenthusiastic the Vatican authorities were about the Council and bitterly resented the intervention of Pope Paul VI in limiting the collegiality of bishops. On the other, he was conscious of the weaknesses of the wholesale concessions to the modern world. He felt that the church, having for centuries opposed the world and in practice having condemned everything that came from it (he believed the suppression of Modernism in the nineteenth century to be an especial tragedy for the church in holding back necessary developments), had now capitulated and accepted uncritically much that secular thought was itself to condemn only a few years later. While in comparison with the great feudal encyclicals from Leo XIII to Pius XII Vatican II was the first great liberal and bourgeois Council, commending to the church the bourgeois virtues of freedom of religion and conscience, tolerance and ecumenism, this happened just at a time when those with a social conscience were criticizing the

Western misuse of liberal values to the detriment of the poor and the inhabitants of the Third World. Vatican II could not have much influence because a completely new set of problems had arisen, and its great proclamation *Gaudium et Spes* seemed very soon to be both naive and dated.

As far as Schillebeeckx is concerned, perhaps the most positive consequence of Vatican II might be seen to be the foundation of *Concilium*, the international theological journal which first appeared in 1965 as a result of the pioneering work of Paul Brand. *Concilium* is important not only for the writings which arise from it but also because of the way in which it maintains regular contact between theologians of different continents, from different cultures, speaking different languages, among other things, by periodical congresses.[5]

From Vatican II onwards a gap inevitably opened up between Edward and his church, not just the hierarchy in Rome but at a more local and personal level. Once the 1968 process began, and Rome was suspicious of him, it was no longer possible for the Dutch bishops to use him as an advisor, though they never abandoned him and he still has the support of Cardinal Alfrink and Cardinal Willebrands, the Primate of Holland, and remains a figure of considerable influence in the Dutch church. About the time when Edward's father was expressing his confidence in Edward vis-à-vis the Pope, the Prior of the Dominican monastery at Louvain where he once taught was commenting, 'We don't see him any more. He used to come a great deal when he was visiting his family in Belgium, but especially after Vatican II he went his own way: a step ahead of everyone else. When I see pictures of him I have to say, "That's not the Schillebeeckx we know".'[6]

Events at the end of the 1960s made a deep impression on him. Student rebellions round about 1968 made him aware of the importance of the approach of the sociologists of the Frankfurt School with their critical theory; travelling through the Americas in 1967 had given him first-hand contact with the Latin American theologians of liberation. All this led him to see his earlier theology as rather conservative; he once even described it as 'stale buns'. It was far too much concentrated on the church as an institution. From now on we can see him moving increasingly away from the church towards the source of Christianity in Jesus and the kingdom of God and the needs of the modern world. Although much that he has written is implicit criticism of the church, that criticism is really directed towards the church only where, as on the question of ministry, the subject is an actual feature of the life of the institutional church. For the rest, his position seems much more to be a steady distancing, which in some respects seems even more damning. In fact he seems to have lost any hope there might have been after Vatican II that the church might renew itself from within; as we shall see, he is not optimistic for the future of the church in Western society; [7] if anywhere, he sees hope here only with the critical 'basic communities'.[8]

In 1966 Edward visited the United States for the first time, and gave a series of lectures there. This was his first taste of a really secularized society (a marked contrast with Holland, where theology is still so much a matter of general public concern), and he saw completely new approaches to the Christian tradition. After his return from America, he became particularly interested in questions of interpretation (more technically known as hermeneutics).[9] This, together with what was emerging from the articles and lectures of the previous years (he had written no major book since 1969) and all the events of the tumultuous 1960s, political as well as theology, was the first step towards the major theological event in his life. The writing of *Jesus* was coming into sight. So far modern biblical scholarship and its findings had played very little part in his published writing, but now he determined to remedy his lack of knowledge in this area, setting out to master all the relevant literature on his subject, which anyone at all familiar with its extent will know to be a more than Herculean task. For three or four years after 1969, study of the interpretation of the New Testament, particularly the Synoptic Gospels, was his major preoccupation. He cut down on his public engagements, and popular though he was with television companies, even resisted their pressing calls.

We shall be looking at the significance of *Jesus* in a later chapter; at this point it is enough to note the vigorous response it received: acclaim by the wider public and the theological world and disapproval from the Vatican. The details of the latter's response are known well enough, and the events leading up to the summons of Schillebeeckx to Rome in December 1979 have been more than adequately chronicled. They need not concern us here, except to note that Schillebeeckx is quite convinced that his own theology is an orthodox development from the earlier mainstream Christian tradition; it differs in being expressed in other language and other concepts. By the end of this book you will be able to judge for yourself.

Whether official silence on his writings will continue is perhaps open to question, since his book on *Ministry* (Dutch 1980, English 1981) has caused almost greater concern in Vatican circles than *Jesus*, a reaction which was prophesied on its publication in Holland and has been the subject of regular public comment since. For while restatements of doctrines, even restatement of the significance of the person of Jesus, need not necessarily have any tangible consequences, a restatement of the doctrine of the priesthood at a time when the Roman Catholic church is in crisis over it because of the decline in numbers in the great religious orders, the questioning of celibacy and the lack of priests to celebrate the eucharist, especially among the rapidly expanding populations of Third World countries, of necessity calls for a revolution in current attitudes and practices. Challenging church structures is inevitably more controversial than preaching 'heresy'.[10]

During the 1970s Schillebeeckx's social concerns also led to his being involved in public discussion of a number of ethical and political issues in Holland, ranging from abortion to the formation of a new left-wing political party. However, the public issue on which he has expressed his views most strongly is that of nuclear weapons: he finds it quite impossible to distinguish between the questions of possession and use of them and therefore regards the deterrent theory as morally untenable. This led to some controversy on the occasion of one of the two crowning public events of his career, the award to him of the Erasmus Prize in September 1982. The Erasmus Prize has been awarded annually since 1958 to 'individuals or institutions who have made important contributions to European culture in respect of culture, social sciences or other social questions'; although it had previously been given to Martin Buber and Romano Guardini, as philosophers and humanists respectively, Schillebeeckx was the first to receive it as a theologian; others honoured had been philosophers, artists, politicians and journalists. The jury judged that his theology was both a confirmation of the values of European culture and a contribution to the criticism of that culture, a fact which is evident not only from the content of his acceptance speech but also from the reported establishment reaction to it, which was said to be far from favourable.

In his acceptance speech he included an apt quotation from the fifteenth-century philosopher Giovanni Pico della Mirandola, which seemed to him to be an uncanny prophecy of the future of Christian humanism in all its later forms:

> God was pleased to create man as a being whose form is indefinite. He put him at the centre of the universe and said to him: 'We have not assigned you a place to dwell in, a particular appearance; we have not given you a special gift, O Adam, so that you can appropriate for yourself any dwelling place, any appearance, any gift that you desire, according to your own powers and your own views. As to the other creatures, their nature obeys laws which we have prescribed for them and which mark out their limits. As for you, no impassable frontier will bar your way, but you will determine your own nature in accordance with your own free will, to which I have entrusted your destiny. We have not created you celestial or terrestrial, mortal or immortal; you shall be your own free sculptor and poet of your own image, to give yourself freely the form in which you desire to live.'[11]

He goes on to point out how the reckless and selfish Western concern for self-realization has not brought salvation either to individuals or to society. We have exploited people from other parts of the world and by our domination of nature have actually come to pose a threat to human survival through pollution, scientific manipulation and the nuclear arms race. In all this science is not to blame, but mankind, and as the year 2000 approaches we are forced to ask whether the question of human salvation is to retain any meaning at all. If religion has anything at all to say here, that religion must be concern for man in the world, a religion which begins from faith in a liberating God and is interested in human beings in their specific historical and social context. Whatever one thinks of contemporary theologians, he concludes, one thing should be granted them: in their commitment both to mysticism and to politics they are trying to discover the human face of God and, starting from there, to revive hope in a society, a humanity with a more human face.

With Schillebeeckx, one is never allowed to forget that theology goes hand in hand with cultural, political, ethical and ecological concerns. And similarly, one is never allowed to forget that Christian involvement in these concerns must not amount to a mere religious veneer on top of secular approaches and actions. It must be a deeply thought out and professional activity. That he brought home at a second great public event. He retired officially from his professorial chair in Nijmegen on 1 September 1982, but did not give the traditional 'last lecture' until ll February 1983, an occasion on which he was honoured by being made a Commander of the Order of Orange-Nassau, the highest civil honour in Holland. This time, as we shall see later, his concern was quite specifically theological, connected above all with hermeneutics, the science of interpretation, which has been his ongoing preoccupation since Vatican II and that first visit to America.

Theologizing, or theological understanding, is always a second, reflective enterprise, based on what is experienced, confessed and thought within believing Christian communities. However, theological reflection can sometimes outstrip the churches' preaching or prepare for future developments in that preaching, for the simple reason that theology has to be concerned not only with what happens today, which is always limited, but also with the broad spectrum of the whole of the Christian tradition, with its Christian experiences reaching back over many social and cultural changes. As a theologian I seek to give priority to the 'instinct of faith' within the Christian communities, nurtured on the Bible.[12]

How Edward Schillebeeckx has sought to combine these focal points of faithfulness to the tradition and concern for our world will occupy us for the rest of the book.

3

Christ the Sacrament

Over the past decade and more, liturgical revision has been a major preoccupation of all the churches, Catholic and Protestant alike. In the Roman Catholic church the Latin Mass has given place to worship in the vernacular, and in the Anglican and Protestant churches new prayer books and lectionaries produced with modernized language to go alongside the new versions of the Bible have come into almost universal use, while new hymnbooks containing substantial alterations to both words and music have contributed to the break with the past. Despite the often incongruous effect which is produced, the internal arrangements of churches have been changed to provide for an altar at which the president celebrates facing the congregation.

Many church traditions have followed Roman Catholicism in making the eucharist the focal point of worship each Sunday, and it has become an important symbol of the nature of the church, the character of its community and its commitment to a life of sacrifice for the outside world.

Such changes, particularly in connection with the eucharist, have given rise to a considerable amount of devotional literature and material which explains the new developments, but on the whole only at a superficial level. What is notably lacking is material which explains just how sacraments are to be understood and what is the fundamental nature of the eucharist in a world in which more than words and ceremonial have changed since the earlier days of Christianity. After all, down the centuries over which the eucharist has been celebrated the human race has experienced cultural, social and scientific revolutions, and it would be rash to assume that while in other respects our understanding had altered, in the case of the eucharist we had a constant handed down unaltered from earliest times.

This question might seem to be most urgent for the Catholic tradition, in which at the eucharist the focal point of attention has seemed to be concentrated on the bread and wine, elements which are held to undergo a miraculous transformation at their consecration. The doctrinal position is buttressed by the widespread liturgical practice of veneration of the consecrated host at services like Benediction and memories of popular beliefs of its magical powers or the dangers which arise from its profanation. The Roman Catholic doctrine in question, that of transsubstantiation, according to which the substance of the bread and wine are supposed to be changed into the body and blood of Christ while the accidents, i.e. the outward appearances and characteristics, remain the same, has thus led to a stress on a real presence of Christ understood to come about in an almost physical form through consecration of the elements, and celebration of the eucharist has at times looked like a procedure aimed at achieving this real presence almost regardless of the attitudes of those present. As we shall see in a later chapter, it is also associated with quite definite views about the nature of ministry.[1]

It is therefore important to note that in his first major study Schillebeeckx went to the heart of the matter by considering, a decade before Vatican II and the changes which it introduced, not the outward details of the eucharist but its very nature and character. This study, *De sacramentele heilseconomie*, was published as early as 1952; it has never been translated, but a shorter, revised and non-technical version of its conclusions did appear in Holland in 1959, and was translated into English under the title *Christ the Sacrament*. Perhaps because it is a second version, in structure and approach it is perhaps the most satisfactory of all Schillebeeckx's works, so it provides a good place from which to begin.

As we read the book now, it is important to remember that we are going back to the thinking of Edward Schillebeeckx the lecturer at Louvain, influenced by his encounters with existentialism in Paris, his reading still almost exclusively dominated by the Catholic tradition, with an enormous amount of his development still ahead of him. Because of that, what we read can hardly be taken to be his current views (on more than one occasion he has expressed a wish to rewrite in different terms the major *De sacramentele heilsecon-*

omie, and so detailed comment on them would be both inappropriate and pointless. However, it is important to become acclimatized to the Schillebeeckx approach, so that straightforward exposition of the work followed by a few comments at the end is as good a way as any to begin.

Christ the Sacrament, the shortened form of the original Dutch title, is not as illuminating as the full version, *Christ the Sacrament of the Encounter with God* (itself derived from an even fuller version *Encounter with Christ the Sacrament of the Encounter with God*), which immediately brings out the perspective from which Schillebeeckx approaches the question. If we forget the importance of personal encounter within the sphere of human experience, a sphere which also includes the sacramental world, then there is a risk that the sacraments become mechanical processes. Traditional theology, Schillebeeckx is concerned to argue, does not always bring out sufficiently well the distinction between the mere physical presence of natural objects and the unique character of conscious human reality and human existence. The personal call which the living God addresses to man in his particular situation often seems endangered by a reduction of religious life to an impersonal level. The sacraments, in particular, have been treated too exclusively in terms of an impersonal cause-effect relationship, leading to the impression that receiving grace in them is largely a passive affair.

That sets out the problem; but how is it to be solved? If you are concerned to justify an approach to the sacraments in terms of encounter without going against the official teaching of the church (and at this stage Schillebeeckx gives no evidence whatsoever that he feels at all unhappy with the basis of that teaching – the kingdom of God has not yet come to exert its pressure and make the sphere of the church seem too narrow), where do you begin?

Schillebeeckx begins at the beginning: with creation – and with St Augustine. Augustine divided the gradual coming into being of the church into three great phases, and Schillebeeckx follows this pattern. First came the church of the devout heathen. Here God called, and his call was dimly echoed. Those who listened with an upright heart dimly suspected that a redeeming God was concerned for their salvation. But this experience of grace either remained hidden in the depths of the human heart or at best was expressed in a motley collection of religious forms and aspirations, in which it is extremely difficult to distinguish the true from the false. Nevertheless, pagan religious society, revitalized by great religious leaders, was a providential sketch of the true church that was to come, and its attempts to give form to its religious aspirations bear witness to the truth that grace is never given just inwardly, but confronts us also in visible shape.

Next came the beginnings of a special divine revelation which happened first of all in Israel. It developed dialectically, that is, out of the dialogue struggle between God and his people, in fidelity and infidelity. Through all the ups and downs of the history of Israel God sought to lead his people to a final and definitive faithfulness, and its visible religion, its faithful people, its cult, sacraments, sacrifices and priesthood formed a church which was already a visible presence of grace. However, in this existential two-way struggle between God who calls and man who resists, God's calling seemed to fail; Israel was not faithful until God himself raised up a man Jesus, in whom was concentrated the entirety of mankind's vocation to faithfulness. Here at last the dialogue between God and man, which had broken down so often in the history of the Jewish people, was made perfect. To quote words of Schillebeeckx from his exposition of the theme elsewhere:

> In a single person both elements are fulfilled: the invitation, and the reply of perfect fidelity, and in such a way that both the invitation and the response constitute the completed revelation of God. The man Jesus is not only the one sent by the Holy Trinity, he is also the one called to be the representative of all humanity. He is not only the visible embodiment of God's wooing of man, but also the representation and highest fulfilment of the human response of love to God's courtship. Jesus, the free man, who in his humanity reveals to us the divine invitation of love, is at the same time, as man, the person who in the name of all of us and as our representative accepts this invitation. As head of redeemed humanity, he is in a sense the whole of mankind. That is why it is possible for his sacrifice to be at the same time our redemption. Our personal communion with God can only take place, explicitly or implicitly, by an interpersonal relationship with the man Jesus.[2]

But how does that interpersonal relationship come about? For

Schillebeeckx, Christ himself is the church, an invisible communion in grace with the living God manifested in visible human form. Moreover, because the saving acts of the man Jesus are performed by a divine person, they have a divine power to save. And because this divine power to save appears to us in visible form, the saving activity of Jesus is sacramental, because the sacrament is a divine communication of salvation in such a way that the bringing of this salvation takes on visible bodily form. The shorthand way of putting all this is to say that Jesus is *the* sacrament, the primordial sacrament, and that affirmation gives the book its title and its ultimate foundation. As Schillebeeckx goes on to say, for Jesus' contemporaries to be approached personally by him was an invitation to a personal encounter with the life-giving God, because personally that man was the Son of God. So human encounter with Jesus is the sacrament of the encounter of God.

For the disciples, the times of their close companionship with Jesus were the high points of their experience. One might think particularly of the Last Supper, or the glance of Jesus at Peter which moved him to tears. Here Jesus made his presence an intensely vivid reality, while the disciples experienced their spiritual bond with him more deeply than ever. On both sides it was the physical personal encounter which was the point at which the spiritual encounter culminated, and man's experience of God took on a highly personal form.

Human encounter with Jesus is the sacrament of the encounter of God. But there is a problem. Jesus has disappeared from the visible horizon of our life. How do we encounter the glorified and risen Christ, who has vanished from our sight? Men who are dead can exercise no direct influence on us; as men they have passed from our world and will not return to it. 'Mutual human availability is possible only in and through man's corporeality.'[3] Do we now therefore have to be content to live our lives without any bodily encounter with Christ? Must our encounter with him be only in the spiritual contact of faith? Yes, in part. But the problem posed above is not insoluble. For first, Christ is not just dead, but dead and risen, and secondly, he represents God reaching down to us for our salvation in an initiative which is constant. Given this, we can still conceive of a more bodily encounter with him. The basis of any such encounter must involve first, the resurrection, and secondly an initiative on his part which makes his heavenly corporeality in some way visible in our earthly sphere. Now he can only make himself visibly present to earthbound men by taking up earthly non-glorified realities into his glorified saving activity. And that is what the sacraments are, the face of redemption turned visibly towards us so that in them we are truly able to encounter the living Christ. Furthermore, they are always a personal action of the Lord.

When Christ the primordial sacrament left our earth, Schillebeeckx continues, a different pattern had to become operative. This is the pattern of the 'separated sacraments'. While none of the twelve apostles who went around with the earthly Jesus was baptized, Paul, who never met him, was. The sacrament thus bridges the gap between the Christ of heaven and unglorified humanity and makes possible a reciprocal human encounter between Christ and unglorified humanity, even after the ascension.

Again, Schillebeeckx has elsewhere put this in moving words, at one point reminiscent of a vital feature of his childhood, which are worth quoting here because the original is no longer very accessible:

> From behind the cloud of his glorification, behind which he withdraws from our still earthly eyes, the Lord in his visible church reaches for earthly, unglorified elements which for that very reason are visible to us, elements as unpretentious as the child in the crib [one is here reminded of that very first of Schillebeeckx's religious experiences]: a little bread and wine, oil and water, a fatherly hand upon the forehead, in order to make his heavenly, saving act effectively present to us here and now. The church's sacraments are, therefore, our quasi-bodily encounters with the transfigured man Jesus, a veiled contact with the Lord but nonetheless one which is concretely human in the full sense because both body and soul are involved, The eucharist is the crowning point of this actual encounter with Christ.[4]

In moving on from the primordial sacrament to the separated sacraments we also move on from the earthly Jesus to the church. It is impossible, Schillebeeckx argues, to think of Jesus as man and messiah without his redemptive community. As representative of fallen mankind Jesus had to win this community to himself and make it the redeemed people of God. That means that through his messianic life as servant of God and by his death he gives rise to the church of which he is head; in Augustine's words, 'Christ dies that the church might be born.' The church is not just a means of salvation but the visible realization of salvation. It is the body of the Lord; consequently it can even be given the the same designation as Jesus himself and be called the primordial sacrament. (At this point we need not go into Schillebeeckx's discussion of how the twofold function of Christ becomes visible in the distinction within the community between the hierarchy and the faithful; if the argument holds at all, it belongs rather with the question of ministry, which we shall be considering later. However, it is important to note that at this point he does establish the distinction between hierarchy and laity, as also between the institutional and the charismatic.)

As primordial sacrament, the church performs visible actions which are sacramental. This sacramental activity extends more widely than the 'seven sacraments', but it of course includes them:

> Each sacrament is the personal saving act of the risen Christ himself, but realized in the visible form of an official act of the church. In other words, a sacrament is the saving action of Christ in the visible form of an ecclesial action [this less familiar adjective is chosen here to avoid the restrictive connotations of 'ecclesiastical']. The validity of a sacrament is therefore simply its authenticity as an act of the church as such. The essential reality that in one or other of seven possible ways is outwardly expressed in the reception of each of the sacraments is consequently the entry into living contact with the visible church as the earthly mystery of Christ in heaven. To receive the sacraments of the church in faith is therefore the same thing as to encounter Christ himself.[5]

So far, the argument has concentrated on the Godward side of the encounter which takes place between Christ and mankind in the sacraments. But an authentic encounter is two-sided. It is therefore time for Schillebeeckx to introduce this other side, by pointing out that the sacrament does not make visible only Christ's divine love for men but also his human love for God into which the members of his body are caught up. The sacrament not only makes present on earth Christ's mystery of saving worship but also the church's inward identification of itself in faith, hope and love with this mystery of worship. Because the sacraments are actions of the church their administration never concerns the recipient alone, even if it may concern him or her personally. Even in the sacrament of penance, where the communal element might seem virtually to have been lost, the grace of forgiveness of sins is assured to the penitent sinner because the church, together with Christ, is praying for him. 'The church is busy on the penitent's behalf long before he kneels down in the confessional.'[6]

Although we have been going along with the argument on Schillebeeckx's terms, it must never be forgotten that he is interpreting the sacraments in line with the teaching of the church and that what he says has to accord with that. To talk in terms of encounter inevitably raises questions about other ways in which Catholic doctrine talks about sacraments and the grace they confer. For example, the Council of Trent stated that the sacraments confer grace *ex opere operato*, signifying, in Schillebeeckx's words, that there is an 'infallible connection between the mystery of worship and the bestowal of grace',[7] a position often understood to suggest magic. To think of sacramental grace in terms of magic, Schillebeeckx argues, is to turn the whole matter upside down: that the bestowal of grace does not depend on the sanctity of the minister or the faith of the recipient means that Christ remains free, sovereign and independent with regard to any human merit whatsoever. *Ex opere operato* and 'in the power of the mystery of Christ' mean the same thing. And the sacraments are a real mystery: when we are talking about their efficacy we are not talking about some cause-effect relationship; what they mean is that 'when the human prayer of the glorified Son of God is sacramentally realized among us in a truly religious act on the part of the church, through the sending of the Spirit by Christ, grace is really bestowed upon us in the same sacrament by the Father of mercies'.[8]

Although the church's sacraments are humanly speaking quite clearly separate from Christ, Schillebeeckx is always concerned to identify them as closely as possible with Christ's person. He stresses the way in which material things of the world around us are taken and humanized through our own corporeality, so that in union with our bodies they become an expression of our spiritual thoughts. It is in connection with that that he introduces the comparison with the jazz drummer that we looked at in the first chapter of this book.[9] To make doubly sure that the point goes home, he then goes on to illustrate it in another way.

It is only when a person's love is manifested in some telling and appealing gesture, through which it becomes possible for me to enter into this love, that I become personally confronted with this love for me. The flowers which I have an agency deliver to friends overseas on their wedding day are to them the concrete presence of my love and friendship; the concrete interpetation of my love; love in a form that is visible. This, but in infinitely greater measure, is the case in the sacraments too. For the proof Christ gives us of his love is not turned into a lifeless thing. It is not merely an indication of an absent love which nevertheless in the indication somehow becomes present. The sacramental proof and token of love makes a living unity with the human saving will of Christ in heaven. Because this is a personal act of God the Son – even though done in human form – it transcends time and space, and therefore in the literal sense of the word, like the soul in the body, become incarnate in the outward rite.[10]

The sacraments are signs, but they are compelling signs, inviting gestures, the making of an offer. Between humans, the firm handshake naturally draws the firm grip in reply. One human glance, one human smile, can do wonders in our lives and by it we can be made into new people who in the strength of the love which comes to them in that small token can begin life anew, apparently with powers that were not there before. How much more then, can a smile of the man Jesus, God's smile, change our whole life? And that is what the sacraments are: the expression of love, fully aware of all the possible consequences.

There is no need to consider in so much detail the next stage of the discussion, which is concerned with what conditions are necessary for a sacrament to be authentic. Here Schillebeeckx affirms and then discusses four:

1. The sacramental symbolic action must have the twofold liturgical structure of act and word.

2. The minister performing the sacramental action must have the intention of doing what the church does.

3. The recipient must have the intention of receiving the sacrament.

4. There must be the institution of the sacraments by Christ.

He goes into a number of specific questions which arise, like the necessary minimum for the minister's act to be a sacrament and the administration of sacraments to infants. However, where the non-Catholic reader, and particularly the reader familiar with modern New Testament criticism will follow him with great interest is in his affirmation that Christ himself indicated the sevenfold direction of sacramental meaning.

Of course he realizes the complexity of the problem. 'For example,' he remarks, 'Christ did not say to his Apostles, even by mere implication, "Today I am instituting confirmation, which you are to adminster in this fashion." '[11] His argument is a sophisticated *tour de force*, taking into account the occurrence of degrees of change in the administration of sacraments, which even includes a footnote on different kinds of bread (ending with the caustic comment that many of the manuals, confusing the different levels of the issues involved, give the impression that a theologian, in order to determine the essence of a sacrament, must among other things be thoroughly conversant with all the different species of grain and know all about viniculture).[12] Whether it works is rather a different matter.

Given that the argument all along has been that the sacraments are to be interpreted in terms of encounter with Christ, it would seem most appropriate to end our survey of the book by seeing what Schillebeeckx has to say about the way in which the individual believer encounters Christ in them. We have seen that the sacraments are held to be effective apart from the faith of the believer and that the believer is always to be seen in the context of the whole church. However, there is more to be added to that. It is only when the beginnings of some religious ardour are present in the believer who is to receive the sacrament that his sharing in the worship of the church will be a worthy sacramental expression of his inner spirit; unless that happens the sacrament cannot develop into a real mutual encounter.

Beyond that, the sacraments are certainly no easier path to holiness, as though they dispense us from part of the religious striving asked of us in our summons to reconciliation or our quest for God. They are above all significant as moments of supreme ardour in everyday life. Just as in everyday life there are decisive or momentous actions in which we express ourselves more intensively and everyday actions in which our freedom is expressed to a lesser degree, so too there are decisive or momentous actions (the sacraments), and everyday acts of grace. Unless we approach the sacraments as momentous actions, they are all too likely to become flat and be reduced to a soulless formalism. If they are approached for what they are, we shall find our spirits raised to new heights.

'The sacramental way,' he concludes, 'is our hidden road to Emmaus, on which we are accompanied by our Lord. And even though we are not able to see him, we are conscious of his concealed presence near us, for when he addresses us through his sacraments, our hearts, intent on his word, burn with longing and we turn at once to Christian action – in the words of the evangelist: "Were not our hearts burning within us while he spoke to us on the road?" '[12]

That last quotation of Luke 24.32 is worth noting. Between 1957, when he ended *Christ the Sacrament*, and 1983, when he gave his final lecture, Schillebeeckx learnt a great deal and a great deal happened to him. But when he came to England immediately after that final lecture, and preached in St James's, Piccadilly, the verse still had a prominent place. This time it was quoted not against a background of sacramental teaching, but in a discussion of the resurrection and its meaning for the modern world. A question to ask, he suggested, was whether Christians were still on the Emmaus road, indeed whether others who were not Christians were accompanying them, in that while they found much in the Christian faith problematical, they nevertheless felt a warmth in their hearts, a 'burning', which was to be seen as the calling of Christ within them (perhaps like St Augustine's restless heart). The whole context had changed, but the passage still retained its capacity to evoke new thoughts. And that seems to be an important feature of Schillebeeckx's whole approach.

Summarizing quite a complicated book in a few pages cannot produce an exact précis of its argument; there will inevitably be distortions in an abbreviated account. However, that was not the point. I have simply attempted to provide some guidelines which will help readers, particularly readers unfamiliar with Schillebeeckx, to find their way through *Christ the Sacrament* for themselves. There they will find a much more nuanced argument which takes into account points that I have not been able to touch on and which answers questions which may well have occurred to them. However, there is one point which is not discussed in the book, though it appeared right at the beginning of this chapter. Against the background of this discussion of the sacraments as encounter, what is to be said about the Roman Catholic doctrine of transsubstantiation, which focusses so much on the element of bread and wine and at first sight seems to be saying something quite different? That question is not discussed in *Christ the Sacrament* because another complete book is devoted to it, in English somewhat misleadingly called *The Eucharist*.

The Eucharist is a relatively short work, written some time afterwards, and takes a quite different approach from *Christ the Sacrament*. One reason for that – which is not immediately obvious from the text – is that it was an attempt to defend new Dutch interpretations of transsubstantiation when they were being condemned by an encyclical from Rome. Hence its different focus. It is concerned with the teachings of the Council of Trent, and because that Council defined the doctrine of transsubstantiation, what it affirmed has to be examined in some detail and the crucial question is how particular texts from the past are to be understood. However, the opening remarks are still presented in a broad context.

Schillebeeckx begins by reminding us that the question of 'new theology' is in no way a modern one. It had already arisen in the thirteenth century in the persons of modernists like Albertus Magnus (to whom we shall return in a later chapter) and Thomas Aquinas, who replaced the mediaeval realism of bleeding hosts – illustrated to marvellous effect in the murals in the chapel on the north side of the sanctuary of the cathedral in Orvieto – by a 'non-sensualistic' approach, which was more of a 'scientific faith'. If we find some modern developments disturbing, we should reflect on the tensions which a change of this magnitude produced. Both approaches were in fact after the same thing, an appropriate affirmation of the presence of Christ in the eucharist, but the differences between them were enormous. When such changes take place, those persuaded of the validity of the new approach will find themselves living alongside those who still hold to the old views, and this position may go on for centuries. Hence patience and understanding is called for. In view of what was to happen a decade after this book appeared, it is worth recalling what Schillebeeckx went on to say next, after pointing out that today conditions are much more explosive than they were in the past.

Faith is, thank God, no longer simply a question for those who are theologians. In our time faith and theology have become news for the press, and this has led to the development of a new ethical situation for the theologian. He can no longer pursue his theological enquiries in detachment from the question how ordinary people in the church are going to interpret what he has written. The fact that this new interpretation must perhaps be regarded as necessary is not the final thing to be considered. The new ethical situation lays upon the theologian the obligation of so formulating the new interpretation that the Catholic faithful may be enabled to recover their deepest insights concerning the faith and may not be simply shocked. He must also beware of giving any cause for enthusiastic disciples heedlessly abandoning the deepest Catholic sense of the faith simply because they have missed the point of the new and 'obvious' interpretation. It is of course true that alarm can never be avoided entirely and that the fear of causing a certain amount of disturbance is no reason for remaining silent. No one can foresee all the reactions – justified and unjustified – there will be to what he says or writes. But our contemporary situation demands that the practice of theology should be carried on in a genuinely ascetical way as a work of mercy. If this is not his attitude, the theologian, whose aim must be to make the mystery or the dogmas of faith speak to us in our life here and now, will have missed his finest opportunities and in fact have repudiated the basic intention with which he set out.[13]

After the statement about doctrinal criticism which we met in the first chapter,[14] he then looks at what the Council of Trent said about transsubstantiation. Immediately before doing so, however, he makes another point which is not often taken as well as this. One often finds people distinguishing between the wording of a dogma and its essence as though one can dress a dogma up in words and strip it of words again like a child dressing and undressing its doll. However, a distinction of that kind can be made only retrospectively. When confronted with what may be for us an outmoded way of thinking we may feel able to distinguish between the wording and what was 'really meant'. But for Christians of the time when the dogma was formulated, this was impossible. That dogma stood or fell by its wording; they could not put it otherwise, and that is why the church would press for a specific idea or specific wording. And that too is why as time goes on there is nothing for it but a constant reinterpretation of the Bible and doctrine, as the intellectual climate and perspective in which they are seen constantly change.

At the Council of Trent, the theologians were concerned to maintain that Christ was present in a specific and distinctive eucharistic way in the eucharist. They could maintain this only by working with the Aristotelian concepts of substance and accidents, and therefore the way in which they affirmed the presence of Christ took the form of a doctrine of transsubstantiation, in which the substance of the bread and wine in the eucharist changed, but the accidents still remained the same (what has been summarized here in a short paragraph Schillebeeckx establishes by careful discussion of the conciliar texts).

However, Aristotelian philosophy is only one way of seeking to comprehend reality, and there have been many others over the centuries, each of them historically conditioned. The early view of the presence of Christ seems to have been more dynamic. Change in a thing could mean that other powers seized it and took possession of it: Irenaeus could describe a Christian as someone whose flesh had been seized by the pneuma, the spirit. As material things could be seen as being without qualities, capable of investing themselves with whatever qualities the Creator desired, change in the context of the eucharist could mean that the Logos took possession of the bread and wine and made them his own body and blood, almost as an extension of the hypostatic union in the incarnation. Furthermore, as the word transsubstantiation seems to be connected with the word *superstantialis* used in Latin translations of the Matthaean version of the Lord's Prayer, it may well have been chosen among other things for its echo of biblical language, and though Tridentine dogma clearly understands the word in Aristotelian terms, they need not necessarily be associated with that conceptuality.

Given that there have been various ways up to and including Tridentine dogma of affirming the real presence of Christ in the eucharist, all of them historically conditioned, the way for a new interpretation is open. However, that interpretation must not contradict the original, inviolable datum of faith which these formula-

tions have attempted to express, nor minimize it. The remainder of
the book surveys modern restatements of the doctrine of transsubstantiation and develops Schillebeeckx's own view, a summary of
which here would be too complex to be illuminating and is in any
case not strictly relevant to our purpose.

Critical comments were ruled out from the beginning in this essentially expository account, because *Christ the Sacrament* in particular
comes from a very different period of Schillebeeckx's thought.
However, in view of what is to come it is worth noting four specific
features of the book.

First, the Bible plays only a minor, almost a cosmetic role, in the
work as a whole. Compared with Schillebeeckx's more recent
writings, the biblical exegesis is primitive, and is very much at the
service of the doctrinal element in the work. The Jesus of the
encounter is very much the Christ of Chalcedon in biblical garb
rather than the Jesus of Nazareth whom we shall be looking at in the
next chapter.

Secondly, for all its critical element and its new interpretation,
from our present perspective *Christ the Sacrament* now reads for a
good deal of the time as a work of Catholic devotion. Here is still the
Schillebeeckx whom the sisters admire rather than the man who
commands the attention of people outside the church as well as in.

Thirdly, following on from that, it is a book with a limited scope,
leaving unanswered so many questions that one would now ask that
it would be very difficult to use it these days as a basis for discussion,
as would be possible with later works. It is splendid reading if one
accepts Schillebeeckx and goes along with him to enjoy the ride,
learning a good deal from his company, but as in the long discussion
of the seven 'separated sacraments' – and elsewhere – there is much
that just will not do now.

Finally, *Christ the Sacrament* (and to a lesser degree the later
study *The Eucharist*) is a very tranquil book. There is virtually
nothing in it of the tension which is to be so much a part of later
works, whether arising from Schillebeeckx's favourite idea of 'experiences of contrast' as the source of theological exploration
(though these do in fact put in a brief appearance), from the tension
between tradition and the wider world (there is nothing about
symbolism and sacrament in non-Jewish or Christian religion, for

example) or from the necessarily cross-grained perspective of Dominican spirituality (of which we shall hear more in a later chapter). We are still with the church and awaiting the impact of the kingdom of God.

The Eucharist, from a rather later date, shows some changes from this position, but they are not enormous ones. It is when we look at *Jesus* that we find ourselves in quite a different world.

4

Jesus

Anyone setting out to write a book about Jesus should be aware of
the enormity of their project. They are confronted not only with
source documents the interpretation of which will require a vast
amount of background knowledge and technical expertise if they
are not to fall into the most elementary errors, and with a subject
whose stature can somehow make the most sophisticated attempts
at understanding still seem puny, but also with two hundred years of
failed attempts to penetrate the mystery to any truly profound
depth. Countless authors have written about Jesus without realizing
this, and the most successful of them have even found large audi-
ences, because a book which fails to grasp Jesus in his true dimensions
can still produce a picture which says a good deal about the ideals of
the author and his times, and there is nothing many people like
better than seeing their reflection in a mirror. Countless others have
written scholarly books which have bravely tackled all the technical
problems involved and have somehow lost Jesus, interest and faith
in the process.

Although it, too, ultimately failed in its attempt to portray Jesus
of Nazareth as he was, Albert Schweitzer's classic book *The Quest
of the Historical Jesus*,[1] written at the beginning of this century, is a
marvellous illustration of the difficulties and is required reading for
anyone who might feel that it should be simple to discover all about
the one whose life and death stand at the beginning of the history of
a church and gospel intended for all men and women. Unfortunately,
as both Schweitzer and any history of modern New Testament
criticism will demonstrate, whatever popular faith and devotion –
and more sophisticated fundamentalists and church pastors and
authorities - might want to be the case, any talk about Jesus which

is to bridge the gap between the first-century Jesus of Nazareth and his significance for us and our times has to pass through some very complicated filtering processses before it can arrive at what Schillebeeckx is fond of calling 'a second innocence' and speak to us.

Because it is so important to realize this, before we consider what Schillebeeck says about Jesus, we have to spend a short while looking at the factors which make it necessary to begin this chapter with two such portentous paragraphs and which, incidentally, also make it necessary for Schillebeeckx to spend twenty pages explaining 'Why this book has been written' and another sixty or so on 'Questions of Method, Hermeneutics and Criteria' before he gets down to the real subject matter.

Right down the history of the church there has always been tension between the mainstream church and its practices and others who have felt that the church does not follow the life-style and teaching of Jesus sufficiently seriously, and therefore make more strenuous attempts to live up to the demands of the gospel. There is no room to follow all these attempts here, but we should note how in the second millennium of Christian history a line can be traced from the gospel movements which proliferated in the twelfth century, particularly in the south of France, and other similar 'spiritualist' trends at a later date, through the left wing of the Reformation to the Puritans.[2] This line is particularly important in the long run for modern biblical criticism, because the moral stance of those included in it influenced the Deist movement of the early eighteenth century. With the Deists, criticism of the standards and practices of the church was extended to criticism of the standards and practices recorded in the Bible, so that the movement plays a crucial role in the beginnings of modern biblical criticism, not least in shaping the moral standards by which Christian teaching, including that in the Bible, came to be judged. With them, and through the period of the Enlightenment which followed, discussion of the church and the Bible moved outside the sphere of the church, and a new criterion was used which did not appeal to divine revelation or God-given authority. That was the power of the unaided human reason.

It was against this background that a book was written, so controversial that it was only published after the author's death, which stands at the beginning of Albert Schweitzer's account of the quest of the historical Jesus: *On the Aims of Jesus and his Disciples*, by Hermann Samuel Reimarus (1694-1768), a teacher of oriental languages in Hamburg.[3] Reimarus claimed to be distinguishing what Jesus really said and taught from what he asserted to be the false account in the apostolic writings. The details of Reimarus' arguments need not concern us here; it is his basic standpoint, followed by countless others over the next two centuries, which is significant. The belief that with enough historical research and analysis of the texts of the Gospels one would be able to arrive at a 'historical Jesus' who would prove to be quite different from the Christ taught by the church and a far more suitable inspiration for the contemporary world was the driving force which led to the production of all the nineteenth- (and twentieth-)century lives of Jesus. It introduced a contrast between 'the Jesus of history' and 'the Christ of the church' (which believers were in due course to counter by a less marked distinction between 'the Jesus of history' and 'the Christ of faith'). The former, more hostile, contrast motivated the many sensational accounts of Jesus which have regularly made headlines in the popular press, associating him with secret Jewish movements, magic mushrooms, erotic relationships with Mary Magdalene and even flying saucers; the distinction argued for within the church perhaps came to a climax in the work of the great German existentialist theologian Rudolf Bultmann in the second quarter of this century,[4] and even in scholarly circles is giving way only slowly to a different understanding.

So Schillebeeckx is setting out on a well-trodden path, and it is a tribute to his genius that from the start he can find so many new and important things to say in passing, as well as providing a highly imaginative synthesis of much of modern New Testament scholarship.

Like many before him, he says that his aim in writing *Jesus* is to free Jesus from dogmatics and to follow all that he said and did in his earthly life; to trace how his followers reacted to him and above all how they reacted to his crucifixion. His Foreword optimistically states that he is not going to deal with the often highly sophisticated problems which interest the academic theologian, important though those may be. Believers ask questions which are not normally those which academics want to answer, so there is a need for a book which bridges the gap between the two worlds. His book differs from the nineteenth-century quest that we have been recalling in that he means to discuss the Bible within the context of the church's community and faith, whereas nineteenth-century scholars tried to detach it from its intrinsic connection with the community and faith and to use their critical scholarship to give it independent objective experience outside the church. But that is to ignore the original interplay and bond between the text and its readers, between the Bible and the church's community of faith, and to introduce a divorce between the two. By making the text they studied a passive object over which they could exercise subjective control, the scholars who used their critical approach to search for 'the historical Jesus' in the nineteenth century ran the risk of making their views normative and projecting their ideals on to what they were reading. Moreover, they were speaking only to their own in-group, and not within a community whose life and faith was directly related with their results.

There is no getting away from the need for academic study of the Bible; we have lost our first innocence and there is no way in which we can regain it. But it is possible to strive for a second innocence. As that term has now come up more than once, it calls for some explanation. What Schillebeeckx means by it is something like this. Once we realize that we cannot just naively tell the Gospel stories all over again as they stand, we have to accept the need for quite complex analyses and investigations. However, when these have been carried out and assimilated, we find that over and above the results they produce there is a surplus which is not susceptible to this kind of rational, historical explanation. As we try to put this surplus into words, we find ourselves being led to express it by telling a whole series of perhaps new stories and parables. These may be of deceptive simplicity, but will have a complex background to them; they will meet the demands facing us to maintain our integrity, but will be understandable to those who have not gone through the problems as we have and perhaps are unable to do so. Achieving this 'second innocence' should be the aim of the search for Jesus. The reader prepared to follow this quest should be stimulated by the interplay between the text and his own approach to it to achieve greater personal liberation in the light of the message of the kingdom of God as presented through Jesus. The world in which Jesus lived and its expectations of salvation were very different from ours, but if we follow the course that Schillebeeckx's study suggests we may expect to understand more about the meaning for us today of 'salvation in Jesus, coming to us from God'.

Because *Jesus* is a big book and touches on so many subjects, it is best to approach it with some basic questions in mind, leaving subsidiary matters for closer study at a later date. We have already spent some time on a slightly different approach to the question why the book was written than the one Schillebeeckx provides, but in one way or another all the issues his explanation touches on are covered in here or in subsequent chapters, so that there is no reason to spend further time on them now. It is, however, important to look at his discussion of method and criteria, since these are crucial for what follows. After that we need to look at Schillebeeckx's account of what Jesus said and did, who he believed himself to be, his death and resurrection, and what the early church believed of him as a result. After this we shall be able to reassess what he means to us and the modern world.

Those who are not professional New Testament scholars (even though they may be gifted systematic theologians) and set out to make sense of the the vast and complicated secondary literature on the Gospels and to bring together all the varied and conflicting investigations into a meaningful synthesis immediately come up against an almost intractable problem. There is virtually no biblical passage (scholars call the relatively well-rounded units of which the first three Gospels are composed 'pericopes') over which experts do not disagree among themselves. There is therefore at a scholarly level considerable difference of opinion as to who Jesus really was and what he said and did. That state of affairs cannot be ignored, because more general statements are useless unless they are based on detailed evidence.

Right from the beginning of the tradition there is then a second tension, namely between 'the phenomenon of Jesus', his person, message, ministry and death, and the various expectations of salvation already current apart from him in the culture of his time which influenced – and in some cases may even have distorted - the way in which his significance was interpreted after his death. Because the gospel spread in different cultures among different patterns of expectation, these interpretations may come to vary quite widely. As the churches grew, and grew together, all these different interpretations became fused by means of combinations of the titles which expressed them so that in the end they all become elusive, and because as a result each single one sought to express everything about Jesus, they have tended – as far as later generations are concerned – to end up as meaningless formalized expressions.

All this diversity – in connection with what Jesus said and did, with early interpretations of him, and with the great conglomeration of titles by which he came to be known and worshipped in the church – raises the question, familiar from many modern studies of christology, as to where one can find an element in the search for the meaning of salvation in Jesus which holds the enterprise together. Schillebeeckx's answer is: in the Christian movement itself. He speaks of 'a Christian oneness of experience which does indeed take its unity from its pointing to the one figure of Jesus, while none the less being pluriform in its verbal expression or articulation'.[5] The constant factor is that particular groups of people find final salvation imparted by God in Jesus of Nazareth.

> The constant factor is the changing life of the 'assembly of God' or 'assembly (congregation) of Christ', the community-fashioning experience evoked by the impress Jesus makes and, in the Spirit, goes on making upon his followers, people who have experienced final salvation in Jesus of Nazareth. Priority must be conceded to the actual offer that is Jesus, but this is embedded, vested in the assent of faith on the part of the Christian community we experience as being amidst us in our history. We might say: Jesus was such as to engender precisely that typical reaction of faith which was confirmed by the 'local church' sort of experience.[6]

So far Schillebeeckx has introduced these statements about Jesus and the way in which he was interpreted in the church in the form of assertions without evidence: we have noted the variety of the Gospel statements about Jesus and the difficulties in interpreting them; the different interpretations by the first Christians, and so on. Now it is time to put these generalized statements on a firmer footing. The introductory section thus ends with a survey of the different criteria used in biblical criticism to determine which of the sayings in the Gospels may be attributed to Jesus and which should not. There is no need to consider them in detail here, but the rest of what Schillebeeckx says will make little sense unless it is accepted, as it is by him and virtually all modern New Testament critics, on the basis of complex but quite sound evidence, that the Synoptic Gospels, the prime source for our knowledge of Jesus, contain three main elements:

1. Sayings and actions in the life of Jesus which are related in the Gospels more or less as they occurred.

2. Elements in the life of Jesus already so fused with a viewpoint current in the church that one can only say of them in general terms that a central core derives from Jesus and therefore that historically authentic reminiscences do have a part to play in them.

3. Sayings and actions not spoken or performed by the earthly Jesus in which nevertheless the commmunity, by attributing them to him, expresses what the Lord who is alive in their midst specifically means for them: in other words they show that the earthly Jesus is indeed its norm and criterion.

The key term in the preaching of Jesus is the kingdom of God; elsewhere Schillebeeckx explains this in one of his favourite phrases, by saying that the phrase expresses the conviction that God's cause is man's cause. In fact he does not find it an easy concept to interpret. Whereas on other pages in *Jesus* when he is discussing the New Testament (as indeed in the sequel, *Christ*) chains of biblical references between brackets spring up on nearly every line, here he has to draw attention to their sudden and complete dearth at the very moment when we get to the heart of Jesus' message.

> The reason is that nowhere does Jesus himself seek to explain the notion of 'God's lordly rule' as such; he presupposes it as a concept familiar to his contemporaries; the concrete content of it emerges from his ministry and activity as a whole, his parables and actual conduct.[7]

The long portrayal of the life and teaching of Jesus on which Schillebeeckx now embarks is not dissimilar from that to be found in modern New Testament studies (from which, of course, he has inevitably had to draw them). He demonstrates the shock effect of the parables (interestingly enough partly in a passage which elsewhere appears as a sermon). He shows how Jesus radicalized the law, replacing 'Thus says the Lord' by 'But I say', an approach which was to lead to his death. He accepts that Jesus performed 'mighty acts'.

(The 'miracles' cannot just be passed over in a sentence; the fact that the word is put in quotation marks here follows Schillebeeckx's correct recognition that to talk of miracle stories indicates that we have already moved out of the world in which these stories are set. In the time of Jesus it was generally recognized that some people had paranormal powers, and their number included Jewish rabbis. Jesus' opponents were not troubled by the fact that he did miracles; they wanted to know where his power came from. Schillebeeckx is convinced that Jesus performed at least the miracles involving the driving out of demons and the centurion's servant, while accepting that others may be additions for reasons which we shall consider later, representing the elaboration of Old Testament prophecies which were applied to Jesus.)

Jesus' identification with the outcast and the way in which he joined in meals with those whose morals were thought reprehensible by respectable society (expanded by material which forms another sermon) leads into a demonstration of the way in which Jesus brings freedom from the Law (a section recalling Schillebeeckx's lovely comparison earlier that whereas John comes across to the people as a grim ascetic, in complete harmony with his message of God's approaching and inexorable judgment, as a sort of dirge, Jesus comes over as a song). And we are reminded of how he called God Abba, Father, not least in the Lord's Prayer. Jesus' whole mission is based on a great intimacy with the Father (like Moses, he speaks to God as to a friend). The language in which Schillebeeckx sums up this survey is not the easiest, but at this point it is worth letting him speak in his own words.

All this goes to show that one of the most reliable facts about the life of Jesus is that he broached the subject of God in and through his message of the coming rule [kingdom] of God; and that what this implied was made plain first and foremost through his authentic parables and the issues they raised, namely *metanoia* [change of heart, repentance] and the praxis of God's kingdom. And then this message was given substantive content by Jesus' actions and his way of life; his miracles, his dealings with tax-gatherers and sinners, his offer of salvation from God in fellowship at table with his friends and in his attitude to the Law, sabbath and Temple, and finally in his consorting in fellowship with a more intimate group of disciples. The heart and centre of it all appeared to be the God concerned for humanity. The whole life of Jesus was a 'celebration' of the rule of God and also 'orthopraxis', that is, a praxis in accord with the kingdom of God. The bond between the two – God's rule and orthopraxis – is so intrinsic that in this praxis Jesus recognizes the signs of the coming of God's rule. The living God is the focus of this life.[8]

For all the length of *Jesus*, it devotes remarkably little space to the death of Jesus, apart from pointing out that Jesus embraced death of his own free will and indicating three different motives suggested by the New Testament for this acceptance: that Jesus died the death of a prophetic martyr; that Jesus' death falls within God's plan of salvation as a part of salvation history; and that his death has a saving efficacy by bringing about reconciliation between God and man as a sacrifice. It is as though Jesus' death has to be seen as an inevitable consequence of his life-style and as a prelude to his resurrection. Elsewhere Schillebeeckx enlarges on this by even arguing that we are redeemed 'despite' Jesus' death. We are brought salvation through Jesus by virtue of the fact that he was faithful right to the point of death. He died, but despite this God was not check-mated, for God is greater than death. This means that 'soteriology' is not an area of doctrine which plays a prominent role for Schillebeeckx; he is extremely suspicious of theories which seek to make theoretically more precise the saving significance of Jesus' death since that, he argues, is something that cannot be thematized in any way.

Jesus was executed on the cross, and the group of intimate disciples who had been with him disintegrated because they had betrayed the very thing which had kept them together, namely his person. Yet after a while they came together again in Jesus' name and proclaimed that this same Jesus had risen. What had happened in the meantime? In *Jesus* Schillebeeckx does not answer this question before he has surveyed all the New Testament texts relating directly to the resurrection of Jesus. However, we may move straight to his answer to the question. Here it is important to note just what he says:

> The primary and immediate reply to this cannot be: the reality of the resurrection itself. The resurrection in its eschatological 'eventuality' is after all nowhere recounted in the New Testament; nor of course could it be, because it no longer forms part of our

mundane, human history; it is *qua* reality, meta-empirical and
meta-historical: 'eschatological'. On the other hand a resurrection
about which nothing is said is an event of which nobody knows
anything, for us, naturally, 'non-existent'. Opening up the subject
of a meta-historical resurrection, as in fact is done in the New
Testament, presupposes of course experiential events which are
interpreted as saving acts of God in Christ. It presuppose a
particular experience and an interpretation of it. The question
then becomes: What, after Jesus' death, were the concrete,
experienced events which induced the disciples to proclaim with
such a degree of challenge and cogent witness that Jesus of
Nazareth was actually alive: the coming or risen One?[9]

It cannot, he concludes on the basis of his investigation, be the
resurrection itself, or the empty tomb (because even if that were a
historical fact, theologically it could produce no proof of a resurrection – a vanished corpse is not in itself a resurrection and an actual
bodily resurrection does not call for a vanished corpse) nor yet
'appearances' which as narrated in the tradition already presuppose
belief in the resurrection. So what can it be? His answer, and this is
the element in his book which has proved to be most controversial,
is: a 'conversion process'. What took place between the two events
which are historically accessible to us, the death of Jesus and the
apostles' preaching with new confidence, was the conversion of the
disciples, who came together again despite the scandal of Jesus'
ignominious execution. The fundamental question is therefore what
made such a conversion possible.

The 'conversion' entails a relationship, he argues, both to the
Jesus of Nazareth whom the disciples had let down, and to Jesus the
Christ, to whom they subsequently return. The disciples had fallen
short in their discipleship of Jesus by leaving him in the lurch at the
worst possible moment, but because their relationship with him had
taught them something of his message of the coming rule of God,
which wills the well-being and not the destruction of humankind;
because they had come to know the God of Jesus as a God of
unconditional mercy and forgiveness; because they remembered
the quite special atmosphere of their last meal with him, they could
see their failure in perspective: as a matter of being thrown off
course but not having been deliberately disloyal. Through their

specific experience of forgiveness after Jesus' death, encountered as grace and discussed among themselves, they arrived at the conviction that their Lord was alive. Because they experienced a renewed offer of salvation in their own conversion, they concluded that he must be alive.

> In their experience here and now of 'returning to Jesus' in the renewal of their own life they encounter in the present the grace of Jesus' forgiving; in so doing they experience Jesus as the one who is alive. A dead man does not proffer forgiveness. A present fellowship with Jesus is thus restored. The experience of having their cowardice and want of faith forgiven them, an experience further illuminated by what they were able to remember of the general tenor of Jesus' life on earth, thus became the matrix in which faith in the risen One was brought to birth. They all of a sudden 'saw' it.[10]

This account of the resurrection has been thought to fail to do justice to what Christian tradition had always asserted. How, on the basis of apparently such an insignificant happening, can the church go on singing triumphant Easter hymns? Is this all that there really was to the glorious resurrection? The protests in some quarters became more and more vehement. However, it is important to listen carefully to what Schillebeeckx is saying before getting too hot under the clerical collar. (He was so careful to avoid misunderstanding that when he felt that the first two Dutch editions of *Jesus* might give a misleading impression he added an extra section, incorporated in all the translations, and then went back to the question again in his *Interim Report*.)[11]

He does seem to have wanted his presentation in one way to have had a shock effect. He clearly feels that the popular form of the traditional understanding of the resurrection current in the churches – there was a tomb with a body in it which suddenly became empty; Jesus was *seen* by his followers after his death in a form which was not an apparation; therefore he is Lord of the world, Alleluia! – leaves much unsaid and unexplained, and that in modern times a different presentation which is open to more constructive discussion is called for if we are to do justice to the reality with which the church's doctrine of the resurrection of Jesus is concerned. On the popular view it is all too easy for the resurrection to function as an 'event in itself', without any saving relevance for humanity. And there needs to be a reaction against that, so that people do not suppose that they can catch sight of the resurrection of Jesus outside the act of faith, and therefore outside an experience of faith. But he certainly does not – and does not intend to – minimize the doctrine of the resurrection.

This becomes clear if we go back over his statements again, particularly in the light of subsequent comments, and read them as he means them to be read.

First, he asserts quite bluntly that belief in the Jesus who is risen and lives with God and among us cannot be founded on an empty tomb as such, nor as such on the visual elements which there may have been in 'appearances' of Jesus. He explains why this is the case at some length, and those who still find this insistence puzzling should go on to read some of the other contemporary literature on resurrection faith, where they will find precisely the same point being made in different ways.[12] However – and here Schillebeeckx is in fact much more conservative than some alternative interpretations – he stresses that what he has just said need not of itself necessarily imply that both the tomb and the resurrection visions were not a historical reality.

Secondly, in talking about 'a process of conversion', he does not mean to reduce the tradition that Jesus appeared to his followers to the fact that in reflecting on what Jesus had said and done the disciples came to certain vivid realizations about his person and significance. To understand what happened to the disciples we have to put ourselves back in their world.

In view of the nature of man in ancient culture, it does not seem to me at all necessary to deny visual elements in the Easter experience of the first Christians. Easter grace seized their heart and senses, and their senses through heart and spirit. It would indeed be a mark of one-sided rationality if we were to remove all emotional aspects from this particular experience. Concomitant, even visual effects seem to me to have been ready to hand for these men within their culture, while the existing model itself already points to them; in other words, even the models usually come into being only on the basis of particular historical experiences. However, it is not a question of these concomitant visual phenomena; at most they are an emotional sign of what really overwhelmed the disciples: the experience of Jesus' new saving presence in the midst of his own people on earth.

Is not the experience of the presence of the Lord and thus the unique conversion experience which the disciples had after Jesus' death and through which they became Christians by grace not of itself also a very emotive, solemn event? If anywhere, here was an inexpressible experience of the divine, the basis of the formation of the new community, in the strength of the risen Jesus who is present among his disciples now gathered together again. This renewed gathering of the disciples who were scattered after Jesus' death *is* the fruit of the new presence of the now glorified Jesus.[13]

It is impossible here to explore all the dimensions of Schillebeeckx's understanding of the resurrection of Jesus, but it should already be clear that his is a serious, positive attempt to do justice to both the subjective and the objective elements of the resurrection together, in a way which can be understood in the contemporary world. And it is based on the view that in what we call the resurrection something did indeed happen to Jesus as a result of the response of God to his life which gave him eternal life in which we too shall share. The more Schillebeeckx's approach is explored in all its complexity, the more it compels admiration. We shall, in fact, be able to set it in a much wider context when in a later chapter we have explored what Schillebeeckx means by talking about 'salvation from God'.

The next theme of *Jesus* is the way in which the earliest Christians came to interpret Jesus after his death. Reconstructing the beliefs of the earliest churches before the times of the New Testament writings is not an easy matter, because the only evidence we have is that of the New Testament itself. That we can go back to the period between Jesus and the New Testament is possible at all only because of the nature of the Gospels: we have seen earlier that they came into being through an interaction between the remembered words and actions of Jesus and the early church's response to them, which included reshaping the words and accounts of the actions and even attributing new words and actions to Jesus in the light of who they believed him to be. By looking at the process of reshaping we can gain some idea of the concerns of the communities through which the stories of Jesus passed; in addition, study of the letters of Paul sheds some light on the communities with which he was associated and other traditions and practices with which he came into contact. It has to be admitted, however, that reconstruction of this kind is at best extremely hypothetical, and probably leads to no more than illuminating possibilities. Given the lack of evidence, no scholar can be asked for more.

So, as far as we are able to discover, how did the earliest communities pass on their message about Jesus? Different communities did this in different ways, and right from the start Schillebeeckx draws attention to the diversity in primitive Christianity. The two first communities he identifies are that behind the material in the Synoptic Gospels common to Matthew and Luke (long referred to by New Testament scholars as Q [= *Quelle*, German for source], as this material is seen as a source drawn upon by those two Gospels), which he refers to as the Q community, and the community standing behind the Gospel of Mark. These earliest communities continued to proclaim Jesus' message that the kingdom of God was imminent; in other words they continued just what he had been doing. The Q community, Schillebeeckx argues somewhat controversially, does not seem to have proclaimed the resurrection of Jesus explicitly, though it had an implicit message of the heavenly Jesus and his continuing work in the community; by contrast the community behind Mark believes Jesus to be absent from his sorrowing and suffering church, and waits longingly for him to appear at his *parousia*, his eschatological coming. That is why there is no account of any 'appearances' of Jesus in the original text of Mark: Jesus will appear only at the *parousia* and not before. The atmosphere in these communities is summed up in their Aramaic prayer *maranatha*, 'Come, Lord', so that Schillebeeckx often talks of a *parousia* christology or a *maranatha* christology in this connection.

Against this background, he sees Jesus as having first been understood as the 'eschatological prophet'. After his interpretation of the resurrection, the choice of this term to describe Jesus proved to be the most controversial feature of the book, and was among the factors leading him to write an *Interim Report*, bringing out points in *Jesus* and *Christ* which he felt had not been understood sufficiently clearly. This, he says, is the model which was found to fit Jesus most closely and he even goes so far as to say that if the model had not already existed, the impression Jesus had made on his disciples during his ministry would have obliged them to invent it.

The idea of the 'eschatological prophet', Schillebeeckx explains, goes back to the Deuteronomic tradition in the Old Testament. By the time of the Babylonian exile, with Deutero-Isaiah (Isa.40-55), the idea and expectation of this prophet, who is closely connected with Moses, the suffering servant of God, has been fused with the notion of the 'innocent sufferer' (which comes from elsewhere), to produce a picture of the prophet who prepares the way of the Lord. These are the terms in which Jesus was first interpreted.

This interpretation called forth a good deal of criticism because a number of theologians who reviewed *Jesus* when it first came out felt that it had too 'low' a view of Jesus and that by giving it pride of place, as he did, in his account, Schillebeeckx was bringing down all the other honorific titles later given to Jesus to that level. It seemed a far cry from Jesus the Son of God to Jesus the eschatological prophet. We shall be looking at this issue shortly; for the moment it is enough to note Schillebeeckx's retort to those who find 'eschatological prophet' inadequate, that they have not thought hard enough about the significance of the word 'eschatological':

> Certainly in the New Testament, the term eschatological prophet implies that this prophet is significant for the whole history of the world, and significant for the whole of subsequent history, no matter how Jesus and his followers may have conceived of this ongoing history [i.e. whether or not they thought that the end of the world would come soon]. Thus eschatological prophet means a prophet who claims to bring a definitive message which applies to the whole of history. It is clear from texts from the [earliest] tradition that Jesus himself was convinced of this, and even more that he attributed world-historical significance to his person.[14]

If, Schillebeeckx goes on, the future or the historical influence of a person is part of the identity of that person, then that is uniquely true of Jesus, since today's living Christian communities are not just accidentally part of the complete identity of Jesus. Here the historical influence of Jesus begins to belong to his identity in a very special way, for which the first Christians chose 'eschatological prophet' as a description. 'In and through what he is, says and does, Jesus points beyond himself to the whole ongoing history of mankind as the coming of God's kingdom.' (Incidentally, the understanding of Jesus as the eschatological prophet also explains why more miracles have been probably attributed to him than is historically likely. When the eschatological prophet came, he was expected to perform the miracles mentioned in the texts of Isaiah, giving the blind sight, making the lame walk and so on. So when people believed that Jesus was the eschatological prophet, they attributed these miracles to him.)

Taking up a famous phrase from the writings of the great German Protestant New Testament scholar Ernst Käsemann, who had argued that apocalyptic is 'the mother of all Christianity',[15] Schillebeeckx goes on to argue that '*parousia* christology [i.e. the kind of christology which we have just been considering, including the notion of the eschatological prophet] is the mother of all Christianity'.[16] What underlies Christian belief is the conviction that despite all appearances to the contrary, the kingdom of God is still coming. In that, and in the disciples' perception that Jesus' understanding of God as Father, coupled with the whole of his life-work, lies the source of their recognition of the character and role of Jesus.

That may seem rather different from what the New Testament now seems to be telling us about Jesus. The reason is that as the gospel spread more widely, other ways of responding to Jesus made themselves felt. To *maranatha* christologies Schillebeeckx adds three more. One approach sees Jesus as the wonder worker, a figure somewhat reminiscent of Solomon, who does not do wonders for his own profit but for the salvation of others and for that reason is abused publicly, though later vindicated. Another associates him with divine Wisdom, which as Judaism developed had taken on an independent existence in personified form; Jesus could be either identified with that wisdom or be seen as having been sent by it. Or finally, he could be seen as the crucified one whom God had raised from the dead, an approach in which great stress came to be laid on the resurrection.

Schillebeeckx sees these four approaches as four different credal strands or models, representing the way in which different groups found definitive meaning and purpose, definitive salvation in Jesus. Each in its own way, they represent particular viewpoints and expectations which stirred people at the time. Though different, they find their unity in the person of Jesus and his persisting eschatological relevance. Schillebeeckx takes pains to stress that while we can assign these different models differing degrees of importance, we cannot arrange them in chronological order. Because earliest Christianity was diverse, what may have come to be believed in a particular group at a later stage need not necessarily have been a late creation of that community; it may have long been part of the belief of a community elsewhere and only come to be integrated into another tradition as a result of mutual exploration of beliefs. In essentials, this is the main thrust of Schillebeeckx's study of the New Testament evidence for the person of Jesus and the first responses to him. However, it is by no means the end of the book. For here, we have to remember, is no academic investigation but the necessary prelude to answering the question that is raised in the title of the last part of *Jesus*: Who do we say that he is?

As we have already seen, when working on this last section Schillebeeckx realized that to give an adequate answer called for a further volume. As a result, he was confronted with quite an acute problem. How was the first volume to end? At one stage he had contemplated abandoning the fourth part altogether and making *Jesus* end at virtually the point we have reached, but changed his mind at the last moment because he felt that to end the book without some kind of christological synthesis would have raised all kinds of fundamental questions. So he decided to insert a provisional systematic section which some readers have felt suddenly brings them with a jolt from the explorations they have been following in previous pages back to the familiar world of classical christology.

The reasons why he felt obliged to put in this section are worth studying particularly by those who have wanted to call him 'dissident', and testify to his pastoral responsibility as a theologian. The section

in fact merely interrupts the work of providing a bridge from academic theology to the contemporary belief of Christians in the modern world which is reserved for the second Jesus book. I have deliberately made up my mind to pay the price, for two reasons. First, I was well aware that had this book been published without a short reflection on the Chalcedonian Definition, so that many readers, believers, would have been confronted only with the development from the very beginning of New Testament belief,

I would have been guilty of disturbing them in a quite irresponsible way. The fact that now even a few not particularly 'conservative' theologians – if it makes sense to use this terminology here – have fundamentally misunderstood the book, shows that my fear of causing illegitimate unrest among believers was justified, although at the same time I accept that there are also cases where it is legitimate to cause unrest among Christian believers. Secondly, because there would be a chance that many people might not be able to grasp the importance I attach, for theological reasons, to a historical and genetic study of the apostolic faith without any reflection on the Council of Chalcedon. Thus I was well aware that the consistent and gradual development of the christological programme which I had undertaken was interrupted through this insertion. However, I feel that 'the mercifulness of faith' must also be a mark of the theologian. I may be criticized here, perhaps rightly, but I gladly accept this criticism for the sake of the cause which the Christian theologian represents.[17]

So *Jesus* does not really come to an end. It looks forward to its sequel *Christ*, and an exploration of grace and salvation as the way in which our life and history can become one of liberation, deliverance and emancipation.

There is no doubt that *Jesus* is a watershed in Schillebeeckx's theology, as we have already seen.[18] And that raises the question whether there was a particular point at which he decided to write the book, a point at which he was conscious that his theology was taking on new characteristics and focussing on a particular issue. Asked directly, he is evasive, and for an answer one has to go to an account, already mentioned above,[19] of the pattern of the academic lectures which he gave during his time at Nijmegen. From that it is clear that, unlike say Barth, his books did not arise immediately out of his lecturing. However, certain interests – he began by lecturing regularly on eschatology, was preoccupied with the question of resurrection, connecting both of these closely with christology, and lectured on hermeneutics[20] every year from 1966 onwards - all came together and fused as the subject matter for a substantial book after a decade of writing no more than articles.[21] And so *Jesus* appeared. We shall see something more of the background to it in Chapter 9.

We could go on to follow through the development of the

argument in *Christ* on the same lines as that of *Jesus*, but that is probably not the best way forward. As I indicated earlier, *Christ* is a much more diverse book than *Jesus*, and covers a very wide range of questions. So in Chapter 6 these questions will be covered by a thematic approach, rather than through the analysis of a particular text. Before that, however, for a change of scene we move to Schillebeeckx's views on ministry.

5

Ministry and Basic Communities

If nothing else, it seems that the mere passage of time is going to bring enormous changes to accepted patterns of ministry in the Roman Catholic church. The evidence for such a bold statement lies in the statistics about the ministry produced regularly, which indicate that so many men are leaving the priesthood through death, retirement or resignation and not being replaced that short of a miracle the number of Roman Catholic priests ordained in accordance with the traditional pattern and traditional requirements will be inadequate to maintain eucharistic worship and carry on their other pastoral responsibilities in the church.[1]

According to the Statistical Yearbook of the Church, in 1976 about half the parishes and missionary posts throughout the world had no resident priest; in many cases the communities concerned amounted to thousands of baptized persons. This situation is getting worse, since almost everywhere in the world church the number of baptized persons is growing in relation to the number of priests. In many areas the absolute number of priests is declining or their average age is rising ominously; even where the number of priests and seminarians is actually increasing, this increase is not enough to maintain the ratio within communities of believers because of the even greater rise in the birthrate. Moreover, for example in South America, and in other areas too, many if not the majority of priests are religious who often tend to be foreigners. Their numbers will not be maintained because of the fall in vocations to the religious orders, above all in Spain. Detailed figures are available to substantiate all these statements.[2]

If we look more closely at the situation in North America and in Europe it emerges that in the United States, between 1966 and 1978 the number of priests active in the pastoral ministry declined by 16% (about 10,000) and the number of seminarians declined by 25,000; in many dioceses the average age of the clergy is increasing rapidly. In French-speaking Canada, where the Catholics are concentrated, the number of priests declined by an even greater percentage over the same period and the average age rose. In Europe, the number of priests everywhere is decreasing rapidly, and their average age is increasing to a disturbing degree. With the exception of Poland and perhaps Yugoslavia, in recent years the number of those who have died or left the active ministry has exceeded the number of those ordained. When one looks at actual replacement percentages, i.e. the percentage of vacancies arising for whatever reason which are actually filled, the position becomes crystal clear. In 1975, in Poland this rate was 175.5 and in Yugoslavia 160.2, but comparatively fewer overall numbers are involved. The replacement rate in Europe was highest in Great Britain with 73.4; Italy had 50.2, Ireland 45.3, Spain 35.9 and West Germany 34; in France the rate was 17.9, in Belgium 15.5 and in Holland a mere 7.7.

What this means for the church is already becoming very clear in Belgium and Holland, where the crisis is most severe. In Holland a halving of the number of diocesan priests in just over a decade and a fall of a third in the number of religious was bound to make itself felt. The pattern so far has been to fill the gaps in the numbers of parochial clergy with religious, but as their numbers are also declining fast, this cannot be a long-term measure.

Clearly developments of this kind worldwide indicate more than superficial problems in the Roman Catholic Church; in any organization whatsoever they would have to be seen as evidence of deep-seated malaise, and whatever the church may *also* be, it is not least an organization. However, here is not the place to go into the problems felt not only by clergy throughout the world and the burdens consequently borne by the more sympathetic of their bishops and superiors, nor to pursue the stories of vast empty seminaries and religious houses. One way or another, if the present trend continues it will force change, and the important thing for the church is not to find itself in a position in which moves within it are dictated by pressure of circumstances rather than by the demands of the gospel of the kingdom of God (and although these two things are often conveniently confused in attempts to justify particular lines of action they are by no means necessarily identical). That is why Edward Schillebeeckx has for a long time been particularly concerned with the question of ministry and the form that it should take in the modern world. The preface to his book on the subject mentions about twenty earlier articles written over a period of twenty-five years. It concludes with ominous words:

> A theologian knows that what he says will not be welcome to everyone. However, convinced as he is of the liberating power of the truth (including the historical truth) which he is in honour bound to pursue, he does not have the right to impose censorship in advance on his own insights: he is obliged to make public the results of his investigation. Historical arguments can be countered only by historical arguments to the contrary. *Nijmegen, 10 August 1980, the anniversary of my ordination to the priesthood*[3]

In looking at *Ministry* we shall not in fact find ourselves directly launched into controversy, though this is arguably the most controversial book Schillebeeckx has written. Its great strength and the conviction which it carries arises out of a very thorough *historical* investigation, as usual based on an awe-inspiring amount of research, which occupies a good deal of the book and its impressive footnotes. Book though it now is, it has been formed around four articles published separately, which accounts for the different levels of writing and degrees of technicality. What it actually amounts to structurally is a cross section of views of ministry at different periods of the church, compared with one another and set off against the situation of the ministry of the church today.

Varied the form may be, ranging from a discussion of the biblical evidence for the form of the earliest communities, through a quite technical examination of the change in conceptions of the priesthood in the Middle Ages, via alternative communities to an evaluation of the Synod of Bishops held in 1971 and a letter sent by Latin American priests to John Paul II in July 1980, but more than in any other of Schillebeeckx's books it is possible to set down an impressive argument point by point which gathers great strength as it goes along. I shall list the points in summary form before we go on to look at them in more detail.

1. The community has a right to priests.

2. The decisive element in ministry is the recognition of the minister by the community.

3. Problems arise when there is a shift of emphasis so that ministry is no longer related to the church, but priestly power is associated with the celebration of the eucharist.

4. A church order which has grown up through history can hinder what it was originally intended to ensure.

5. A church order maintained over a period of change can become a new ideology in the eyes of which necessary new developments are 'illegal'.

6. But there is contemporary evidence of a wealth of promising experiments the development of which is often hindered by the absence of a male celibate priest.

7. When you look back at the New Testament, its patterns of ministry are very like these new developments.

8. After the Decrees of Vatican II, which have changed the basis on which celibacy is seen as a necessary condition for the priesthood, it is possible and legitimate to ask whether celibacy is indeed mandatory for priests.

9. Whatever the theology may be, in practice the church is extremely reluctant to change the rule of celibacy.

10. Where do we go from here?

The scene with which Schillebeeckx opens this most challenging of books – challenging because the argument outlined above is made to emerge directly from a historical survey – will be familiar to those who are acquainted with the picture of the early churches which arises from New Testament criticism on the basis of a very careful reading of all the books of the New Testament. Those coming to it with a background of the assumptions about developments from Christ to the mainstream church of the third and fourth centuries AD, which tend to be based on a mixture of uncritical tradition, legend, projection of later developments back on to the past and mere wishful thinking, are in for a rude shock.

Apart from apostleship or the 'apostolate' the Christian communities did not receive any kind of church order from the hands of Jesus when he still shared our earthly history. Furthermore, 'the Twelve' were the symbol of the approaching eschatological community of God, which originally was not yet organized for a long-term earthly history. This primary, fundamental datum of the New Testament must already make us very cautious; we must not be led astray into speaking too casually about divine ordinances and particular dispositions in respect of the community and its leaders or ministry.[4]

The New Testament, he continues, bears witness to two successive periods: the time of the 'apostles' and the post-apostolic period. The Twelve were a symbol of Israel's twelve patriarchs and tribes, and of the whole of Israel as a sign of the eschatological community of mankind. Their origin more than probably goes back to Jesus (those who find this statement strangely cautious should try making out a list of 'the Twelve' directly from the Gospel record). They are known as 'apostles', but in addition to them the earliest Christian idea of apostleship includes those who had come to follow Jesus before the founding of the first communities or before the newly-founded communities had been built up. In addition to them were 'prophets', spirit-inspired believers who seem to have travelled a good deal among the new communities. The Twelve and the other apostles and prophets believed themselves to have been sent by their dead but risen Lord in the cause of Jesus to continue his proclamation of the coming kingdom of God. The first communities received the faith from them on the basis of the personal experience of Jesus which most of them had had. When this first generation died, the communities were conscious of how much they owed their character to their founders, being proud of their 'apostolic foundation'. This became a description regularly applied to the church thereafter, but at a later date : in the same way as e.g. the followers of Benedict came to call themselves Benedictines.

The early Christian communities were founded by people proclaiming the gospel of Jesus who were constantly on the move. So when such missionary apostles moved on, as we see from Paul's letters, their functions of leadership and co-ordination were taken over by obvious and spontaneous leaders, male and female, in the various communities. These leaders do not as yet have fixed designations, and it is dangerous to read back later conditions into the earliest church. There was obvious variety; it is interesting that while we know that government by a group of elders (presbyters) is very old – James the brother of the Lord was associated with such a group – Paul never mentions presbyters in his letters.

Ministry only arose as a theological question for the communities after the death of the first generation, above all the apostles and prophets. What was to be done next? A desire to stress that the original work was still continuing is evident from the way in which a number of letters in the New Testament (like the Pastoral Epistles) are written as though by Paul, whereas we can now be virtually sure that they are the work of a later generation. But this desire for continuity of the original apostolic work was not a kind of 'apostolic succession' of ministers only. How could it be, when there was as yet no fixed and established form of ministry? It was the responsibility of the whole of the community.

Towards the end of the first century we begin to come across technical terms for ministers: presbyters, *episcopoi* (overseers) and deacons, but on the evidence that we have it is impossible to tell how they relate to one another and what their precise responsibilities are. For example, presbyters are sometimes called *episcopoi*. In addition we still find prophets, and alongside them teachers.

Information about the circumstances Schillebeeckx has just been describing is taken from the New Testament letters where it can be found without much difficulty. It can be supplemented, on a rather less secure basis, by reading between the lines of the Gospels and other passages not directly concerned with ministry. As the Gospels were written not just to preserve the memory of Jesus and his teaching, but to serve as expressions of a living relationship between Christ and his church in which the church felt free to interpret, enlarge, expand and even supply sayings of its Lord, they can be read not only in a quest for Jesus but also in a quest for the character of the early church; indeed, as we have already found Schillebeeckx arguing, the one of necessity involves the other. Thus, to take one example, the Gospel of Matthew can be seen as coming from a church which followed the old order of prophets and teachers, and there seems even to have been a degree of animosity towards the later introduction of *episcopoi* and *diaconoi*. They also seem to have been under pressure from the developing mainstream church that was not sufficiently tolerant of those communities which did not follow a Pauline direction. The Johannine literature can be seen as bearing witness to communities which had a tendency to turn Gnostic during the second century.

It is striking, he concludes, when surveying the New Testament evidence, that the ministry did not develop from and around the eucharist or the liturgy, but from the apostolic building up of the community through preaching, admonition and leadership. Whatever form it may take, ministry is about the leadership of the community: ministers are pioneers who inspire the community and serve as models by which the whole community can identify the gospel. Who should preside at the eucharist is a secondary matter, though that does not mean that it can be just anyone. Continuity within the church is not so much a matter of a doctrine to be preserved in as pure a state as possible, though that is important, nor of ensuring an unbroken succession of ministers within the church, though theirs is the responsibility for preserving the identity and authenticity of the community in the light of the gospel. What matters is the continuity of 'the story of and about Jesus', being his disciple, following him 'in the most radical way possible, according to the orientation, the inspiration and the stimulus of "the kingdom of God and his righteousness" '.[5]

Here is the basis for the first two of the ten points listed above. The community has an apostolic right to a minister or ministers, and also a right, on the basis of the New Testament mandate, 'Do this in remembrance of me', to the celebration of the eucharist or Lord's Supper. This right has priority over any criteria for admission to the ministry which the church can and may impose on its ministers. Moreover, while in New Testament times there is as yet no organization which extends beyond a particular region, the local communities do not exist in isolation but are bound together in love. Ministry within them is quite evidently a service and not a status, and in the footsteps of Jesus a characteristic of this service is identification with the poor and insignificant.

The scene now changes and we move on to the church in the later centuries of the first Christian millennium. We should pause for a moment over Cyprian, Bishop of Carthage, who was martyred in 258, because he introduced what was to prove an ominous development. Cyprian had a great love for the Old Testament, its language and institutions and was one of the first to apply them to the Christian church. He compared the Christian eucharist with the Old Testament priestly sacrificial language, and calls the minister *sacerdos*, priest. The earlier church had had difficulty in calling their leaders 'priestly': Christ was the great high priest and the church was the priestly people of God, but the leaders are not said to be priests. This introduction of Old Testament ideas in due course not only changed the status of the priest; it was also a factor in the rule of celibacy which seems to have originated among other things from the ancient rules of purity found in Leviticus. Towards the end of the fourth century married priests were required to abstain from sexual intercourse on the night before celebrating the eucharist. As the Western churches began to celebrate the eucharist daily, in practice this abstinence became a permanent condition for married priests and in the twelfth century was turned into a formal law of celibacy. A sixteenth-century theologian, Josse Clichtove (1472-1543), whose views influenced the Council of Trent and continued to shape spiritual literature about the priesthood down to Vatican II, was deeply influenced by Old Testament priestly laws, seeing priesthood in relation to the cult rather than to the community.

In other respects, though, Schillebeeckx is concerned to demonstrate how until the twelfth century the pattern of ministry in the church was much closer to the New Testament pattern than is often supposed. The Council of Chalcedon in 451 ruled that no one was to be 'ordained' unless a community was assigned to him. I.e., only someone who has been called by a particular community to be its pastor and leader authentically receives *ordinatio* (a term left untranslated because it should not be interpreted in the light of later ideas). Here the community maintains its right, by grace, to leaders and takes the initiative. To begin with, the link between the community and its leader was so strong that the leader could not be moved to another community except, say, on compassionate grounds and a minister who for personal reasons ceased to preside over a community returned to being a layman. Nor was the minister first empowered to lead the community and preside over the eucharist because he had received authority through ordination elsewhere: 'the minister appointed by the community already receives, by virtue of his appointment, all the powers which are necessary for the leadership of a Christian community; he receives them from the Holy Spirit via the community.'[6] This recognition by the church, people and leaders, is decisive.

At the eucharist, the whole of the community 'concelebrated'. Concelebration was not what it is now usually taken to be, a celebration of the eucharist by a number of priests. It was a term to describe the fact that the whole of the believing community joined in the celebration of the eucharist, with the priest presiding over them simply as the servant of all (interestingly, when more than one priest did celebrate the eucharist on a particular occasion, the canon was never said by all of them; there was one president and the others remained silent).

In the early church the eucharist could always take place when the community met together because celebrating the eucharist was a function of the community, not the individual. Although Augustine denied the 'laity' any right to preside at the eucharist, even in situations of emergency, his is not the only view; there is evidence of others. Tertullian, at the beginning of the third century, said that where no college of ministers had been appointed the laity must celebrate the eucharist and baptize; in that case they were their own priests, for where two or three are gathered together, there is the church. (In passing, it is worth noting that the dossier in connection with Schillebeeckx's third process pointed out that what Tertullian said was not in accord with the Council of Trent. 'That,' Schillebeeckx retorted, 'is something that you must raise with Tertullian.') Elsewhere, too, it seems that anyone who in particular circumstances was required by the community to preside over it – and thus at the eucharist – became a minister, the authorized leader of the community, by that community's acceptance.

We are still in fact with the first two points of Schillebeeckx's argument. Before we move on to the next ones, which deal with subsequent problems, it is worth our while jumping to his sixth and seventh points, namely that there is a wealth of new experiment in the modern church and that this bears a close similarity to the church of New Testament times and beyond. The argument so far has been that ministry is a function of the community and that celebrating the eucharist is an offering of the worship of the whole community. The whole emphasis in the church should lie in the local communities, with the hierarchy in Rome as a court of last appeal, ensuring that all the churches remain together and do not suffer fragmentation.

Over recent centuries, however, the local church has come almost completely under the power of the Pope who determines everything, including the appointment of bishops. As a result the specific needs and possibilities of the local churches are misunderstood.

Because of the way in which this situation oppresses local churches, alternative communities have sprung up, known as 'basic communities' or 'critical communities', made up of people concerned to follow Jesus but unable to accept the current structures of the church. They exist and are growing all over the world, in Latin America, Italy and Spain, and to a lesser degree in Holland. Schillebeeckx has many contacts with them in Holland and goes to one in Amsterdam where laity and married priests preside at the eucharist.

While Schillebeeckx can sympathize with this on the basis of the evidence we have just considered, he is not happy about it because such practices cannot be church law, even if they have not been condemned. These communities are on the fringe of the church. However, their existence and practices makes clear a very real problem facing the church. On a recent occasion when he was asked to preach in one such community his sermon was on the significance of the Jewish-Christian tradition for the basic community. It also carried an implicit warning to these communities that they should not form a kind of ghetto, or think that they had a licence in the name of the gospel to do whatever they liked; they had to continue in the great Christian tradition.

We shall come back to this later; the next stage in Schillebeeckx's argument to note is his claim that at a particular period in history the concept of the priesthood was changed so that the priest was believed to have an inalienable power which he could exercise on his own, even if the whole of the community is absent – something that Graham Greene described as working like an inoculation.[7]

The change began at the end of the twelfth century and beginning of the thirteenth centuries, at the Third and Fourth Lateran Councils (1179 and 1215). Whereas before this men could be ordained only if they had been put forward by a particular community as minister, now the emphasis shifted from the role of the community to the economic question whether an ordained priest would have financial support. Things were seen in the perspective of the higher levels of a feudal society which also has control in the church. Now, instead of the community putting forward its minister, we have the pattern of a man feeling a priestly calling, making it known, being trained as a priest and ordained, and then waiting for the place to which his bishop will appoint him. The claim of the community, originally an essential element of *ordinatio*, disappears. At the same time it was officially declared (at the Fourth Lateran Council) that the eucharist can be celebrated only by a priest who has been validly and legitimately ordained.

The changes evident here came about, Schillebeeckx indicates, more for non-theological than for theological reasons. The conversion of the barbarians, he wryly comments, made the church barbarian. Bishops who had formerly been free now became the servants of powerful secular lords who built private churches and secured clergy for them at their whim. Even attempts at reform only succeeded in consolidating elements of the feudal system. This involvement in feudalism produced prince bishops, who hardly knew much about church tradition! Moreover, the renaissance of Roman law was decisive on ecclesiology and hence on views of the ministry, detaching as it did the power of leadership from the local church. And in this situation the decisive boundary was no longer that between the believer and the world, marked out by baptism, but – now that virtually everyone was baptized – that between priest and layman, marked out by ordination. Ordination now – and only now – became a sacred rite, giving a man an inalienable status he did not have before, quite apart from his involvement with any church. This opened up the way to practices like private masses, which would have been unthinkable for the early church. Formerly it was the body of Christ, the local community, that the minister had been ordained to preside over; now ordination was endowment with special power in connection with another body, the mystical body of Christ in the eucharist.

Schillebeeckx is concerned to stress that in these developments the church did not intend to break with the church of the first millennium. They were convinced that although new situations had called for new measures, they were still in line with the past. But with the benefit of hindsight we can see that there had indeed been a change which was further accentuated by the pressures of the Reformation. Controversy over the nature of the eucharist led the Council of Trent to be concerned almost exclusively with 'the power of consecration' at the eucharist; in other respects it simply gave official sanction to the *de facto* situation of the time. As a result there came into being the narrow popular view of the Catholic priest which, moreover, is the only view known to many Catholic Christians down to and including the present time. Worse still, it also determines the attitude of the official church towards the present shortage of priests.

> On all sides we hear of new patterns of behaviour which are inspired by that view of the priesthood. Generally speaking they run like this: in view of the growing shortage of priests, let us engage as many lay people as possible in the pastoral work of the church (which in itself is a praiseworthy suggestion). In doing this, let us be loyal to ourselves: let the laity do everything for which they have skills and a charisma. But it is not for them to preside at the eucharist, in the ministry of reconciliation and at least in the sacramental last rites – in other words in sacramental institutions. All this is reserved for those on whom, as celibate candidates for the priesthood, the *sacra potestas*, the sacred power of consecration, has been bestowed.[8]

We have now come to the end of the historical survey and have covered the points in Schillebeeckx's arguments that we passed over when looking at his indications of the wealth of new experiment in alternative forms of community alongside the church. To the existence of those forms of community we must add the facts mentioned at the beginning of the chapter: the acute crisis in the Roman Catholic priesthood throughout the world, indicated by the rapid drop in vocations and the way in which that is increasingly hindering the work of the church, not least in leaving churches without priests and therefore without the possibility of celebrating the eucharist.

As a result of this survey we are left with two different and conflicting pictures of the ministry, one from the first millennium of the church's history and one from the second, and the tension between them is acute. Vatican II, Schillebeeckx points out, ended up with a compromise. It again stressed the community, the church aspect of ministry, and abandoned the loaded word *potestas* for the priest's endowment, preferring terms indicating service, like *ministeria* and *munera*. However, subsequent events distorted this equilibrium. One declaration which shifted the focus back towards the later, second-millennium view was that of the Congregation of the Doctrine of Faith on women in the ministry made in 1976. This document sets out to be a contribution to the struggle for women's liberation, but by leaving women outside all the decision-making authorities in the church it does not get very far. And why are they excluded? Because they cannot preside at the eucharist. Here once again, Schillebeeckx points out, the old connection between church and ministry is again broken in favour of the relationship between the sacred power to celebrate at the eucharist and the ministry. Moreover, Old Testament laws of purity again play an ominous role, bringing up the question of women's 'impurities' in a way which is certainly not Christian.

Why, Schillebeeckx argues, must the fact that, given the culture of the time, Jesus only chose twelve men as apostles, in this connection suddenly acquire a theological significance while at the same time the similar fact that this same Jesus for the most part, and perhaps even entirely, chose only *married* men is not allowed any theological significance, or rather is contradicted by insistence on the law of celibacy? Here is a double standard. Statements made by the church, he concedes, may be correct even when the reasoning behind them is unsound, but that is not the case here. All the arguments converge on the insight that in the case of the exclusion of women from the priesthood, too, we have a purely historically conditioned cultural pattern, understandable in earlier times but problematical in a changed culture which is aware of real discrimination against women. Of course the church authorities must not move too rashly and in a way which might offend those who have not yet become aware of such discrimination and the need to remedy it. But this is rather different from searching around desperately for any old argument in a concern to legitimate the status quo.

To return to the two conflicting views of ministry we have been considering. On the basis of *theological criteria*, Schillebeeckx argues, preference is to be given to the first Christian millennium as a model for the future shape of the church's ministry, albeit in a very different, modern historical context, and in particular to the New Testament period and that before the time of the Council of Nicaea (325), even if in the community of Christ not everything is always possible. The trouble is – and here we come to the ninth of the points listed earlier – not only is it the case that not everything is possible; at the present time very little by way of change is possible at all.

The last chapter makes gloomy reading. The main section in a rather disparate collection of 'perspectives' is an account of the 1971 Synod of Bishops which, to say the least, was an unhappy occasion. We cannot go into all the details here; the unhappiness was caused by a polarization of attitudes among the bishops along the lines of the alternatives that we have been considering above. As a result the synod was unable to achieve anything. Not only the issues we have just been considering, but also differences over the legitimacy of political theology, which we shall be looking at in a later chapter, played their part: 'Anyone who makes a careful study of the tone of the speeches in the debates will sense that the same group of problems lurks everywhere: fear of identifying the message of the gospel with social and political, critical and even revolutionary trends towards liberation.'[9]

Analysing the synod, having noted that the Synod of Dutch Bishops in 1980 simply confirmed its conclusions, Schillebeeckx points to the baneful influence of the doctrinal development which isolated the priest from the church community. Because this was – not entirely correctly – also thought to be the teaching of the Council of Trent, even some of the progressive bishops felt uneasy. And while the church seems determined to defend priestly celibacy come what may, and the Pope's support for the *status quo* is not only powerful but attractive to those who in a troubled world are looking for strong personalities and conservation of the old, change in the future seems unlikely. The existence of the basic communities is only a small sign; Schillebeeckx does not expect them to produce much significant change over the next twenty or thirty years.

But that does not mean that there is not hope for a better situation. 'The stronger the conservatism the greater the resistance,' he commented to one journalist. And even after a depressing council like the Synod of Bishops, the fact remains that support for new tendencies was not expressed just by a few hot-headed priests and theologians, but by virtually half the episcopate of the Roman Catholic Church. Furthermore, in many cases, not least in the United States, the priests and people in the dioceses have more progressive views than their bishops. More may be afoot than can be seen.

But, as Schillebeeckx finally remarks, that is the work of others. His own task is simply to tell the story, in faithfulness to the facts.

A theologian cannot and may not take the place of the pastoral leaders of the church. By virtue of his task as a theologian, in critical service to the church, he has the sometimes painful duty of showing the church authorities whether their approach in fact takes into account all the features of what is actually a very complex set of problems. Here even the theologian in turn stands under the pastoral insight of the leaders of the church, but this must not make him cowardly and prevent him from having his say. He must speak out even when he is convinced that in all probability the church authorities will make other decisions. Each person has his or her own inalienable responsibility for acting honourably and in accord with conscience, aware of the possible consequences which may follow, even for himself, in the church.[10]

Schillebeeckx's views of ministry have not gone unchallenged among his fellow theologians, as well as in Vatican circles. Four questions have been asked:

1. Is not his historical account shaped in such a way as to lead to the conclusions at which he wants to arrive in view of his own experiences of the church today?

2. Does not his account of the past display too high a degree of nostalgia; is he not too naive about earlier situations and developments?

3. Does he not make an artificial break between the first and the second millennia, when in fact the developments he attributes to the second millennium can in fact be found at a much earlier stage?

4. Is not his view of the church community in the past governed by his experience of some contemporary church communities the basis of which is in fact too narrow to be projected into the past and used as a model by which conditions in the church in earlier times may be understood?

Because of this criticism, Schillebeeckx has subsequently qualified his position to some extent in an article which has not yet been translated into English (though the text does end with a brief English summary).[11] Acknowledging that his contrast between ministry in the first millennium and ministry in the second millennium was too schematic, he has now produced a much more differentiated account which above all focusses, as the title of the article indicates, on the social and historical background to shifts in the church's ministry.

This much more sophisticated analysis not only discusses different patterns of ministry in the early churches, depending on their different regional backgrounds, but also follows historical developments in much more detail: the difference between the second and fourth centuries, the transition from the 'classical' period to the early Middle Ages, the emergence of ritualism and of models of priestly life inspired by monasticism, and of a priestly apostolate inspired by the gospel – these are all surveyed.

The new article does not answer all the criticisms which have been made of Schillebeeckx's views on ministry, but they do substantially strengthen his position, and show that he is ready to listen to his own strictures in the Preface to *Ministry*: 'Historical arguments can be countered only by historical arguments to the contrary.' It remains to be seen whether others will challenge his position with the same painstaking thoroughness.

6

Salvation from God

It may be that some people will feel that Schillebeeckx's starting point is far ahead of the position they themselves occupy. He has a firm faith in God, he has committed himself to the religious life, and he is clearly as happy in his commitment as our world allows anyone to be, for all the pressures, tensions and disappointments that he must inevitably experience. How does one begin to get that far, at a time when belief in God is anything but self-evident and we keep being thrown up against the threat of the meaninglessness of everything? A Christian should be able to explain to others why he or she believes, and help those who do not or cannot believe towards having faith.

In the old days, Christian believers, and Catholics most of all, had what they thought to be certainties to appeal to: the Christian tradition, the authority of the church, and natural theology – that is, supposed signs pointing towards the existence of God in the world around them. But that is not the case any more. Modern science in all its varied forms has put such an appeal in question. Any modern court of appeal must be based on a much firmer footing than is provided simply by the legacy of the past. So belief in God has to be thought through again, in terms of the world in which we now live.

In answering the question how we come to believe in God Schillebeeckx would point to two sources. On the one hand there is the whole tradition of the experience of the great Jewish-Christian movement, and on the other the new contemporary experiences of all human beings, whether they are Christians or not. These two sets of experiences must be held in critical correlation; in other words, we also have to analyse our present world, or even worlds of experience; we have to analyse the constant structures of the fundamental Christian experience about which the New Testament and the rest of the Christian tradition of experience speak, and then make a critical comparison between them, taking with the utmost seriousness the points at which the two sets of experience seem to come into conflict. I have used the word 'experience' a great many times in the previous paragraph. That was deliberate, because it plays a crucial role in Schillebeeckx's arguments. The first part of *Christ* is in fact devoted to an extended analysis of experience which is developed further in the *Interim Report*, so that is clearly where we should begin.

Experience, Schillebeecks argues, in a compact, somewhat difficult but nevertheless important statement, is 'a richly nuanced totality in which experience, thought and interpretation run together in the same way as past, present and expectations of the future'.[1] It combines both subjective and objective elements.

> Personal involvement in no way prevents our being open to what encounters us objectively. A man with a musical ear will hear more in a symphony than someone with little feeling for music. Does that mean that he is more subjective? Or is it not rather the case that this subjective capacity is the very element that makes him open to hear all that is to be heard in this symphonic reality? In other words, our real experiences are neither purely objective nor purely subjective. On the one hand, they are not purely subjective; for we cannot simply make something out of something at our whim. At least partially, there is something which is 'given', which we cannot completely manipulate or change; in experience we have an offer of reality. On the other hand, it is not purely objective; for the experience is filled out and coloured by the reminiscences and sensibilities, concepts and longings of the person who has the experience. Thus the irreducible elements of our experience form a totality which already contains interpretation. We experience in the act of interpreting, without being able to draw a neat distinction between the element of experience and the element of interpretation.[2]

All experience is interpreted experience. We can see what that means if we look at a high-point of human life, the experience of being in love. To recognize that one is in love is an intrinsic element of the experience itself, at first an unexpressed interpretation which may then later be reflected on deliberately. When we are in love we know what love is and that it is more than can be expressed at any given moment. Asked to describe what we feel we may have to resort to the language of other people, from the biblical Song of Songs or *Romeo and Juliet* to modern poetry. Our description is not a superfluous elaboration; by applying it to our experience we may make ourselves aware of elements in that experience which had previously escaped us and as a result find the experience deepened.[3]

Now what we discover in everyday life is also the case when we turn to religious experience as it is found in the Bible. For Schillebeeckx, God's revelation of himself follows the course of human experiences. Of course it transcends them, in that it does not simply emerge from subjective human experience, but it can only be perceived in and through a long process of experience. Crucial in that process is what Schillebeeckx regularly refers to as experiences of contrast. There are certain experiences which inevitably come to all men – those of finitude and contingency –in which we cry out for something different. Men and women should not suffer; they should not be hurt and oppressed, they should not be made to weep. And even in their best moments, when they seem almost to begin to transcend their finite natures, as when they reach out to each other in mutual love, there is nevertheless a consciousness of just how fragile this love is, accompanied by a conviction that it should be something more than a transient moment in our humanity.

If we struggle with these negative experiences of contrast, we shall find them productive because we shall be pointed towards the possibility of 'salvation', i.e. a situation in which the negative experiences are remedied and overcome. In fact such experiences play a decisive role in shaping what a people's expectations of salvation may be. Salvation is the search for the reversal of experiences of calamity, suffering, evil and death, and expressions of it will therefore be a mirror image of these afflictions. From a people's views of what goes to make up salvation we can infer the story of their sufferings, even when it is no longer possible for us to trace from elsewhere the precise course those sufferings have taken.

Despite all our negative experience, Schillebeeckx continues, there still seems to be in most people something like a fundamental trust, the trust that in the end all will be well. Those in the English-speaking tradition might like to illustrate this trust from writers as different and as far removed in time as the mystic Julian of Norwich and her vision of the smallness – as small as a hazel nut in the palm of a hand – of everything that is, how God loves it and how in the end 'all shall be well, and all shall be well and all manner of thing shall be well',[4] and the fundamental question asked by the contemporary American sociologist, Peter Berger, in *A Rumour of Angels*. He imagines a child waking in the night, alone in the darkness and terrified by nameless threats. In growing terror, the child calls for its mother who comes bringing light, warmth and reassurance. In whatever way she communicates, her message will be 'Don't be afraid – everything will be all right.' And he asks a question which few people could bring themselves to answer in the affirmative: Is the mother lying?[5]

It seems to be a constant feature of the make-up of men and women, therefore, apparently regardless of their religious background, that they continue to trust that goodness and not evil will have the last word. Of course the ways in which this expectation of salvation, for that is what it is, is expressed, differ widely according to circumstances and historical period. As people change, as their pictures of human nature and the world change, so too does what they experience as salvation and happiness. That helps us to understand the way in which religious ideas of salvation have varied over the centuries.

The trust that things will turn out well in the end brings Schillebeeckx to the conclusion that there is something in mankind which is not of ourselves and which as it were constantly seizes us despite ourselves. That is the power of the creative action of a God who is concerned for salvation. And that salvation finds its final expression, which is our assurance of its ultimate reality, in the person of Jesus. Of course those statements have to be given some justification – after all, that is the point of this particular discussion – and Schillebeeckx gives that justification in terms of an absolutely fundamental issue. Salvation from God in Jesus is the one viable answer for him to the question 'How can you be *sure* that good and not evil will ultimately triumph? How do you know that dreaming of a salvation as a reversal of present circumstances is not just wishful thinking, day-dreaming in a situation which has become intolerable, as was argued by the nineteenth-century philosopher Feuerbach and has been reasserted by others, psychologists and sociologists as well as philosophers, after him?'

This is an important question for Schillebeeckx, because he is aware of just how much utopian dreaming mankind has indulged in. Depending on whether their concerns are radical or conservative, human beings often do either make a selective idealized picture of the past into a model or look for a future in which their longings will be fulfilled. But how do we know whether that future will come about? There is no confirmatory assurance in our history and experience that good will in fact triumph. Schillebeeckx rubs this in with rather a grim illustration. Imagine that a soldier is asked to kill an innocent person. He refuses. Someone else is ordered to take his place and kill the innocent man, and for his disobedience the soldier is killed too. His gesture is ineffective and he is the victim of evil, empirical reality. On what possible grounds could the soldier believe that his action will contribute to the ultimate triumph of God over evil? Hope against hope is splendid, but what is its basis? Can it be man in all his ambiguity?[6]

It is an unpalatable fact, Schillebeeckx points out, that if man is the only source of an ethical value within our history we have no guarantee that good rather than evil will triumph and have the last word. Left-wing groups intent to remedy matters by revolution cannot demonstrate that their approach will succeed; they do not really have an answer to the problem that the situation after 'liberation' will just be a different version of what it was before. History gives us no grounds for an optimistic view of progress. And no happy ending within history can counter the experience of suffering. To that problem, too, he devotes a long discussion in *Christ*.

There is an *excess* of suffering and evil in our history. There is a barbarous excess, for all the explanations and interpretations. There is too much *unmerited* and *senseless* suffering for us to be able to give an ethical, hermeneutical and ontological analysis of our disaster. There is suffering which is not even suffering 'for a good cause', but suffering in which men, without finding meaning for themselves, are simply made the crude victims of an evil cause which serves others. Furthermore, this suffering is the alpha and omega of the whole history of mankind; it is the scarlet thread by which this historical fragment is recognizable as human history: history is a whole world of suffering. Because of their historical extent and their historical density, evil and suffering are the dark fleck in our history, a fleck which no one can remove by an explanation or interpretation which is able to give it an understandable place in a rational and meaningful whole. Or does someone perhaps want to give Buchenwald, Auschwitz or Vietnam (or whatever else) a specific structural place in the divine plan, which, as Christians believe, directs our history? No one, at any rate, who thinks it important to be human and to be treated as a human being will do so. And then we have still not said anything about the unmerited suffering of so many of the nameless among us, in our immediate neighbourhood. Perhaps including our own suffering which we do not understand.[7]

In a moving interview Schillebeeckx described how he had been led to curse at suffering, and how it had thrown him into deep despair, for example when he heard the news of the killing of Archbishop Romero.[8] As well as cursing suffering – which Schillebeeckx points out can itself be a form of prayer to God – we are called to combat it. If on any account, even if we do believe in God, much suffering is quite inexplicable, then the only meaningful reaction is in fact to offer resistance, to act in a way which sets out to turn history to good effect. That is why the word praxis occurs so much in what he says, and why he attaches so much importance, as we shall see in a later chapter, to political theology, which is concerned not only with individuals but also with the structures under which they live.

So far we have been looking for the most part at one of the two sources which Schillebeeckx believes have to be held together critically, namely the experience most of us have of the world in which we live. Analysis of that experience has not demonstrated that there is a God, and in particular the fact of excess suffering presents an agonizing problem to people of whatever beliefs. However, it has shown what human salvation might be, and for those who stand in the Jewish-Christian tradition – and indeed for those to whom they present that tradition – it is possible to see connections between the history and beliefs of the community to which they belong and answers to the fundamental questions of human experience. Moreover, it is possible to argue that the pattern of experiences we have been considering is more easily explained on the basis of a creator God than in any other way.

That we come to talk of 'God' at all is a result of our history. When we are born into the world we are born into a community with a tradition, and many traditions all over the world have long talked about God. The word may be problematical for us today, and if it were not already there before us, we might never arrive at it. However, that is how things are. Now we may not be able to prove God, but the discussion so far should have made it clear that the general phenomenon of religions or believing communities does have a meaningful setting in general human experiences. Even non-believers concede that experience is not a human projection but the given reality of our humanity. The difference between believers and non-believers (between whom in many other respects, as we shall see later, Schillebeeckx makes virtually no distinction) is that whereas non-believers see as the last word, their experience of existing without their choosing to in an alien world, believers can interpet this as the mediation of God's absolute saving presence.

And so we come to Jesus:

All religions are concerned with God, and God is the unknown, the unapproachable One. We do not see him and we do not know him. Now Jesus is the face of God [elsewhere Schillebeeckx even used the phrase 'his smile']. We therefore have to look to the man Jesus and pay attention to his message and his life-style, and follow them out to the death. If we do that, we shall know something of God. So Jesus is the window on God, the manifestation of God among us.

To stress the point again. We cannot approach God himself, except in Jesus, in all his humanity. We only need to look at him to know who God is. That is the only meaning of what people call the incarnation of God in Jesus of Nazareth. We may have no conception of what God is, of what 'he' could be, but we do have some conception of who Jesus is. Therefore Jesus is God's countenance. By stressing the man Jesus you can have some conception of what God is and how he regards human beings. Without Jesus you cannot do that.[9]

For Schillebeeckx, Jesus is supremely important. If we are asked how we know that the expectations of salvation which grow out of negative experiences are not mere projections, wishful thinking, we have to point to Jesus. As we have seen,[10] that is not as straightforward a matter as it might seem. For Jesus has been interpreted in many ways, which will inevitably in themselves include a good deal of wishful thinking and projection. One can enumerate them running down history, from the Christus Victor and Pantocrator, through the Jesus in the manger and the Christ of the Sacred Heart, through the Romantic model of genuine human personality and Christ the King to Jesus the revolutionary and liberator, not to mention some of the more terrible aberrations. Images of Jesus call for critical judgment, including measurement against the time-scale of history: the fact that our age yearns for peace and justice does not mean that we can proclaim Jesus as the great liberator of mankind. But there is a degree of correlation between the two and we need the historical phenomenon of the real Jesus of Nazareth as a touchstone for our own projections.

One cannot go on for ever believing in ideas, Schillebeeckx argues, whether these are abstract or have an existential content. They so often let us down or assume the function of ideologies. He himself can only believe and put his trust in persons (even though he is sometimes betrayed by them as well). Hence faith that all will be well, faith in the salvation which is promised by Christian faith entails not only the personal living presence of the glorified Jesus which – as we have seen – can be misinterpreted in ideological terms, but also a link with his life on earth; for it is precisely that earthly life that has been acknowledged and empowered by God through the resurrection. For Schillebeeckx, a Christianity which lacks the historical Jesus of Nazareth is ultimately vacuous – in fact not Christianity at all.

As we have already discovered, Schillebeeckx sees Jesus as a prophet who had a vision of the kingdom of God which is still an inspiration for us today. But that is not sufficient reason for attaching to him the faith that the church does. We have to see how the gap between the first century and our own day is to be bridged. After all, various other people in history have had similar visions of liberation and the kingdom. How is it to be explained that this man Jesus who lived in a corner of the Middle East unleashed a movement like

Christianity, whereas John the Baptist, his contemporary with a similar message who suffered a similar fate, has disappeared? That is in fact the point at which we left Schillebeeckx at the end of his *Jesus*.

While the personal impact of Jesus may have had something to do with the initial success of the movement to which he gave rise, that cannot be the whole story. Such a personal impact, directly and through the medium of stories told about Jesus, could have been a force for the first few decades, but it cannot have gone on inspiring the church and creating the wealth of its experience century after century down to our present day. The key to the history of the Christian church is therefore a constant interaction between the community and a living reality, not just between the community and a set of stories handed down from the past. Or to put it another way, in the history of the church we are dealing with the same basic experience, interpreted in a variety of ways which are nevertheless essentially the same. And if our present-day manner of thinking, living and acting by Christian faith is structured by the same elements, albeit within our very different world, we shall be sharing the same experience as New Testament Christianity.

But what is this experience which forms the constant, which shaped the community of the earliest churches and is to shape our own? After an extremely long survey of the New Testament evidence which takes up well over half of *Christ*, Schillebeeckx arrives at what he calls four structural elements or principles, the names of which are in fact rather more forbidding than their content.

1. *A basic theological and anthropological principle*. This is the belief that God wills to be salvation for human beings and to realize this salvation through our history in the midst of meaninglessness and the search for meaning. So finding salvation in God coincides with finding our true selves. Salvation from God is concerned with human wholeness and happiness.

2. *Christological mediation*. By this Schillebeeckx means that it is Jesus of Nazareth who is the complete and definitive disclosure of God's starting point. His life and death have value in and of themselves, but above all they have value before God, who identifies himself not only with the ideals and visions of Jesus but also with Jesus' own person, fulfilling the direction of Jesus' life beyond death by his resurrection from the dead.

3. *The message and life-style of the church*. The living community is the only authentic legacy of Jesus, and in the last resort we can only talk about the story of Jesus in terms of the story of the Christian community and its experience. The church does not so much imitate what Jesus did as allow an intense experience of God to have an influence on its new situation.

4. *Eschatological fulfilment*. This is the belief that our story cannot come to fulfilment within the earthly order of our history. As a result Christian experience looks towards a final dénouement beyond the narrow boundaries of our history, of which the resurrection of Christ is a promise. As Schillebeeckx put it in one of his interviews, 'God's heart is greater than the outcome of history, and that is one of the reasons why we may hope for an eternal life in which something new can happen.' The presentation of the last structural element ends with a combination of Schillebeeckx's words with those of the Bible which gives it that emotional power which he can so often command in a unique way. Without the intermediary of human existence and the perception of fragments of salvation which transcend our own human limits, he says, 'the Word of God' is sheer illusion. But in the context of fragmentary experiences of salvation we may rightly speak of the word of God and his promise which transcends all expectations of experience and is yet recognized as what is familiar and evident:

> Behold the dwelling of God is with men. He will dwell with them, and they shall be his people, and God himself will be with them; he will wipe away every tear from their eyes, and death shall be no more, neither shall there be mourning nor crying nor pain any more, for the former things have passed away (Rev.21.3f.).

(This is another of those passages from the New Testament to which Schillebeeckx keeps returning as a key to what he is trying to say.) The New Testament, he concludes, is a narrative version of these four fundamental elements or perspectives of the Christian experience of salvation from God in Jesus the Christ. We do not add our own chapter to the ongoing history which has followed from them, he comments acidly, simply and solely by selling Bibles. Nor are they directly a norm for the contemporary church. But they are models in which we in our own time can make our contribution to the history of the living Jesus.

In this survey of the main theme of Schillebeeckx's account of the nature of salvation from God we have looked at his interpretation of the character of experience, and particularly experiences of negative contrast, and we have looked at his conviction that God is uniquely made known to us in the person of Jesus, the living one to whom the church still responds in its ongoing experience which though constantly different is yet fundamentally the same. We have still to look at his analysis of salvation.

Because, as we saw earlier, the question of salvation is identical with the question of meaning and human fulfilment, that question can be expressed in terms of what it means to be a human being. It is in those terms that Schillebeeckx prefers to discuss it, so the question of what salvation can mean for us today becomes the question 'What is humanity?' What is it to be happy and free, authentic and good, in the light of all our present awareness? What future realization do we long for?

Just as he has looked for structural elements in Christian experience, so here Schillebeeckx gives his answer in terms of a series of seven 'anthropological constants'. He sees these constants as a system of coordinates all of which focus upon personal identity within social culture. They are not specific norms or ethical directives in accordance with which we should ideally live, so much as permanent human impulses and orientations, values and spheres of value.

1. Human beings not only *are* bodies; they also *have* them. As a result they are related to the wider sphere of nature. That means that they are inescapably committed to a concern for ecology and with the physical conditions under which they live.

2. Human personal identity includes relationships with other people. The fact that we never see our own face directly but only the faces of others is a sign of this. Human relationship is more than an 'I-Thou' or 'we' relationship. It includes third parties, and in that fact lies the origin and basis of society. There is no escape into individual inwardness, because that is conditioned by our charcter as beings in society and can also be affected by the next 'constant'.

3. Individuals are related to social and institutional structures. They create these structures, but the structures then take on an independent, objective life of their own. Once independent, the structures give the impression of being unchangeable and natural,

whereas the fact is that they can be and – as time goes on – need to be changed. Again, it is no use saying, like Camus, that while imprisoned by structures human beings can still be inwardly free. As the objectified form of life in society, structures can condition even our 'inwardness' without our being aware of it and therefore cannot be ignored.

4. Human beings are conditioned by time and space. That means that – in contrast to the views of the Enlightenment – in considering human values we are not just concerned with certain necessary or *a priori* truths. Over the course of history, and in some places rather than others, people can discover values which are neither *a priori* nor arbitrary. What is expected of members of Western society, in view of the prosperous circumstances in which they live, need not necessarily apply in other cultures. Furthermore, because human imagination is limited, there will always be scope for those whose history has led them to certain recognitions, not least in the great religious traditions, to pass on those recognitions to others and to realize them in action.

5. Theory must always be accompanied by action, and human action – unlike the activities of the animal world – must always be governed by theory. Unless we want to make our history into a kind of spiritual Darwinism, in which only the power of the strongest prevails (and here Schillebeeckx argues that Western society is too much under the sway of 'utilitarian individualism' which has produced a society in which freedom to pursue one's own aims and interests unhindered is seen as the chief good and individual efforts towards the greatest possible self-realization are expected to be to the private and public welfare of everyone. Endorsed often by the churches and with modern technology at its disposal, this assumption is one of the greatest threats to our world).

6. A 'utopian' element seems to be a permanent feature of human consciousness (we have already considered this above). Without faith in the future, as a ground for hope, human beings lose their identity and end up either in a neurotic state or in the world of horoscopes and superstition. Faith and hope – whatever their content – are therefore part of the 'wholeness' of our humanity.

7. All the six constants mentioned above go together to form a synthesis which makes up the seventh constant. They hold one another in equilibrium and together delineate man's form. Failure

to recognize even one of them affects the whole; it can damage human society and distort it, thus leading to oppression and misery.

Recognition of these constants establishes a pattern for salvation and suggests the way in which Christian salvation can be expressed. As Schillebeeckx sums it up:

> Christian salvation, in the centuries-old biblical tradition called redemption, and meant as salvation from God for men, is concerned with the whole system of co-ordinates in which man can really be man. This salvation – the wholeness of man – cannot just be sought in one or other of these constants, say exclusively in 'ecological appeals', in an exclusive 'be nice to one another', in the exclusive overthrow of an economic system (whether Marxist or capitalist), or in exclusive mystical experiences: 'Alleluia, he is risen!' On the other hand, the synthesis of all this is clearly an 'already now' and a 'not yet'. The way in which human failure and human shortcomings are coped with must be termed a form of 'liberation' (and perhaps its most important form). In that case that might then be the all-embracing 'anthropological constant' in which Jesus the Christ wanted to go before us.[11]

In this way, we can discover from Schillebeeckx an explanation of how salvation from God comes to man. Although much of the argument outlined above can be found in *Christ*, there is no single work, so far as I know, in which Schillebeeckx presents it in this systematic form. Doubtless in the course of the exposition you may have thought of difficulties and problems that are not touched on here. That does not mean that Schillebeeckx has not dealt with them. If his problem, as we saw in the first chapter, is that of presenting everything that he wants to say in a well-ordered form, so that he builds up a case by approaching questions from different perspectives, making sure that he has taken everything relevant into account and as a result leaving the reader to cope with a whole cluster of related studies, not only within a particular volume but spread out over other collections as well, so the problem with any attempt to bring order into all this diversity will be to over-simplify by virtue of the very process of tidying up. However, the course we have followed may prove useful as a main route through Schillebeeckx country, making it possible to embark on more ambitious tours without the risk of losing direction and getting lost.

The account must, of course, remain unfinished, both by the very nature of its subject matter and because Schillebeeckx still proposes to add a third major volume to what he has already written in this connection. We shall be considering in more detail how he believes that salvation may be achieved through action in a study of political theology; and in the last chapter we shall consider the indications Schillebeeckx has given of the contents of his third volume. Before that, however, we shall be turning aside to consider his comments on spirituality, and specifically the spirituality of the religious Order to which he belongs.

7

Spirituality

If I had to single out one piece from everything that Schillebeeckx
has written for the sheer enjoyment that comes from reading it, it
would most certainly be his portrait of Albertus Magnus. If that
sounds unlikely, remember the comment made earlier that Schillebeeckx can make history come alive in the same way as new
approaches to, say Bach and Handel have blown the cobwebs away
and made their works come up in a sparkling new form.[1] However,
pieces of this kind need looking for, and one needs to have some
idea of the delights that can be expected. I doubt whether I would
even have looked at the Albertus Magnus essay had it not been in a
collection of sermons and articles which I translated, and indeed
when asked – before reading it – whether there was any possibility
of shortening a rather long volume, I had blindly suggested it *a priori*
as a candidate for exclusion. Who, apart perhaps from a narrow
circle of Dominicans, would be interested in Albert the Great?

Which only goes to show how wrong I was, and how much is
missed by those whose knowledge of Christianity jumps from the
biblical period and the time of the early church, through the patristic
period ending in the great councils of Nicaea and Chalcedon, to the
Reformation and then on to modern times. There could hardly be
a better introduction to the wealth of personality, knowledge and
achievement to be found in the Middle Ages than in this portrait of
Albertus Magnus, and as one reads it, one feels that whatever the
historical accuracy achieved here - on which I have no competence
to judge – the account comes alive because Schillebeeckx has found
a fellow-figure with whom he can identify closely.

Two columns in the *Oxford Dictionary of the Christian Church*
give a judicious account of Albert's activities. Mediaeval theologian,

philosopher and scientist (c.1200-1280), he is said to have been born near Ulm in south Germany of a noble family and to have studied at the universities of Bologna and Padua, where in 1222 he became a Dominican. He returned to Germany to study and teach theology, and in 1241 was sent to Paris, where Thomas Aquinas was his pupil. Seven years later he was summoned back to Germany again, to Cologne, where he was for a time Provincial of the German province and much in demand as an arbiter in disputes. Various calls took him away from Cologne in subsequent years: he was Bishop of Regensburg for two years, spent time in Rome and preached a crusade, all at papal request; he lived in various other Dominican houses and attended the Council of Lyons. A modern edition of his writings extends to thirty-eight volumes and he was instrumental in introducing Aristotelian philosophy to the West.

So much for the bare bones of an amazing lifetime. But we have to turn to Schillebeeckx to get the feeling that we know the man a little.[2] The family Albert came from did not have the noble, upper-class refinement to be found with Thomas Aquinas; though belonging to one of the better classes of the time, it was one of local officials. Albert spoke the local dialect, and his language is rough and sometimes aggressive. When he was young he went the rounds with his father's servant, keenly observing everything around him. He watched a fight between a swan and an eagle and discovered the real meaning of 'swan song'; he traced the journeys of fish in the Danube and once must have seen a species of whale there, because he even writes about the uses of whale blubber as a medicine. When his father died he went to Padua, uncertain about what to do next. Nature fascinated him and he experienced a great earthquake which wrought havoc throughout northern Italy. Among some of the ruin caused by it people discovered a long-hidden well: it was opened up, a workman went down into it, and died of suffocation. Bystanders blamed the water spirits; Albert explained to them how gases can build up in an enclosed cistern. His attitude was similar at a later date when the whole of north Germany was terrified by a new comet; ignoring the rumours of impending doom he observed the phenomenon with great interest.

Having decided to study the arts, Albert enrolled in the University of Padua, where his life was to be changed by St Dominic's successor, Jordan of Saxony. Jordan had an amazing power to captivate mediaeval students, and as he travelled round the universities his sermons produced numerous candidates for the Dominican Order. Albert at first resisted out of feelings of inadequacy, but Jordan was as good a psychologist as he was preacher, and in one of his sermons happened to analyse Albert's feelings so accurately that he was immediately won over.

His rise to theological fame was meteoric; by his early thirties he had already acquired the reputation of being the greatest scholar in the West, which is why he was chosen by the Order to go to Paris, the academic centre of the world, though he did not even have a doctorate. Having enhanced his reputation even more in Paris, he was summoned back to Germany to strengthen the new theological faculty in Cologne. Theologically he became the *doctor universalis*, a man whom Roger Bacon, his chagrined opponent, had to acknowledge as being – unprecedently – an authority in his lifetime.

A mystic, he wrote commentaries on all the works attributed to the legendary Dionysius the Areopagite through which he influenced Meister Eckhardt and two centuries later Nicolas of Cusa. Much of the latter part of his life, however, was spent as an administrator. In this role he had to do a good deal of travelling, but made good use of the time taken by his journeys to continue studying the world around him. He was not averse to turning aside from his journey to explore mines and examine the ore they produced. As a result, he could analyse minerals and explain how chalk turns into marble, producing remarkable figures in the process. When Cologne cathedral was rebuilt he studied the ancient Roman remains that were uncovered; he knew how to train falcons, taught nurserymen how to improve their crops and farmers how to breed better cattle, and even relieved a convent of a plague of flies.

It was his upright way of living and sense of fairness and justice which made him in such demand as an arbitrator, and which led to his being nominated by the Pope to be Bishop of Regensburg, a problematical see because Albert's predecessor in office had appropriated all the funds for his own use. His superior in the Dominican Order did not want him to go and Albert was pulled in two directions. However, as the Pope's nomination had come first, he accepted that, doing his duty by the Order in staying only a short time in the see and asking to be relieved when its finances were in order and he had found a competent successor. Like so many compromises, however, this was not completely successful and the Order never really forgave him.

Albert clearly appeals to Schillebeeckx not least because he was essentially a pastor. Not for him Thomas Aquinas' view that theology is an academic speciality, even if it does have a pastoral dimension. 'You must study theology,' he would say, 'to become a better Christian.' There were obviously tensions between Albert and his pupil, since Aquinas never once mentions him by name, though he sometimes quotes him word for word. There were also tensions between Albert and other members of his Order, arising not least from his perception of the wider world. At one point his outspoken way of speaking is quite evident: 'There are some people even among us Dominicans whom I would want to call theological obscurantists. They are brute beasts who call down anathemas on things of which they do not have the slightest idea; such people murdered Socrates in former times, drove Plato out of Athens and intrigued to murder Aristotle.'

Such comments will hardly have made him popular, and in fact the last years of his life were very withdrawn. His *joie de vivre* left him, no one would have anything to do with him and he lived the life of a recluse in his cell. The Chronicles of his life tell a sad story. One day an old friend knocked on his door and asked, 'Albert, are you there?' The reply came back, 'No, Albert is no longer here. He used to be here.'

If Schillebeeckx finds much to admire and feel empathy for in Albert's life, at least it seems unlikely that any kind of relationship between the two will extend to that last sorry episode. He has made it very clear that despite the long hours he spends reading and writing, he thrives in the presence of others, especially the young, and could contemplate living in a commune. Albert had long ago said that the search for truth must be teamwork on the part of brothers living together in a brotherly community, and it is quite evident that whatever may be the solitary side to Schillebeeckx's work, he sees what he does as part of a communal effort and his own story as being part of a larger one, in the first instance that of the Order to which he belongs.

That cannot be easy. The issue of *KU Nieuws*, the newspaper of the Catholic University of Nijmegen, published in the week that Schillebeeckx received the Erasmus prize, carried on its front page a picture of him standing by the statue of St Dominic outside the chapel of the Albertinum at Nijmegen where he lives, with under it the headline 'The Last of the Dominicans'. The Albertinum itself, named of course after Albert, is a vast building, constructed during the 1930s with an optimism for the future which was at best short-lived. Some of its long corridors now end in partitions which divide the part still used by the Dominicans from that leased to the university; footsteps echo along empty landings on which open doors reveal vacant and unused rooms. Old photographs of the opening of the house in 1932, displayed for its golden jubilee in 1982, reflect very different conditions and a much larger community. The Dominicans now living there are a tiny group, eating together in one corner of the vast refectory and worshipping together almost as though camped out in part of their enormous chapel. More of them are in the 60-80 than in the 30-50 age group. We have already considered the reasons behind this decline, and there is no need to labour the point here. But it has to be stressed that being a Dominican in Nijmegen at present cannot be an easy life, and it is quite remarkable that men like Schillebeeckx can remain so peaceful and apparently content with their lot, with no torments about what might have been, no regrets for opportunities lost and no depression at a bleak and uncertain future.

The situation, and the way in which it is coped with, comes out in a sermon which Schillebeeckx preached at the celebration of the fiftieth anniversary of the profession of two Dominican brothers and the fortieth anniversary of the ordination of a third (in fact himself, though he does not say so in the text).[3] He has to begin by reminding his congregation that such anniversaries are far more frequent than the first professions of young people or their offering of themselves for some ministry in the church, and that while there is good reason to celebrate the past, the present and the future no longer seem conducive to celebration. He looks firmly at the results the crisis in the Order and in the priesthood has on religious and clergy. They become indifferent. They say, 'We'll see our time out.' They become nostalgic for the past and become more conservative. Or they look for scapegoats.

In the face of all this he goes straight to the nub of the matter. At the heart of the living community of faith, which includes religious Orders and the priesthood, is not so much a message that must be believed as an experience which can in turn become a joyful way in which others may live out their lives, though in different contexts. (And here of course that word 'praxis' appears again!) He affirms his belief that the content of the good news which makes up the gospel is so powerful and surprising that there will always be enough people, men and women, to join it and hand on the flame. 'What we need to remember is that, by grace, the flame keeps burning with the oil of our own lives, if not in Europe, then in Africa or Latin America. After all, Jesus' promises were not limited to Europe.'[4]

Here is one of the major problems, to which we must return in the next chapter. The Western churches, Schillebeeckx affirms, are being enslaved in a subtle way: prosperous Western society is taking them gently by the arm and at the same time fatally hindering them. This produces a crisis in the church, not just because structures are antiquated and authorities insensitive, but because the atmosphere of our society makes everyone technologists. There is much to be said for professionalism, but Western skill and technology and the society to which they lead can reify our spirit, our charisma and our inspiration in the name of rationalization and efficiency, and that can just as well apply to the church. In the meantime non-Christian modern movements show more verve and sense of occasion, inspiration and conviction and even myth and ritual, and that is why they prove so attractive.

In the face of all this, Schillebeeckx echoes Jesus in the Gospel and says, quite simply, 'Don't be afraid'. Anyone who believes that the flame of the gospel will always continue to burn with the oil of the lives of men and women in one or other part of the world can celebrate joyfully without any restraint. After all, there is good news. In a collection of those thematic phrases which we looked at right at the beginning of this book, he reminds his listeners that just as God's concern is man's concern, so God makes man's concern his own, which is the promise of the kingdom of God, the assurance that all will be well. As a result there is something to look forward to, and the celebration is not just in honour of the last of the Mohicans!

Because of his deep-seated faith in God's purpose, Schillebeeckx can contemplate a future which might include the end of the Dominican Order. However, just as he comes from a family to which he is bound not only by ties of kinship but also by a deep affection, so too he has a great love for and commitment to the family which he joined at his profession, and to whose story he has made his own contribution. 'For the most people live by stories,' he has remarked. 'I myself live by my own story. When I became a Dominican I linked my life story with the family story of the Dominicans; as a result, my life story took on a new orientation and I picked up the thread of the story of the Order in my own way. So my own life has become part of the Dominican story: a chapter in it. Through the story of the Order I have attained my own identity. Stories of the Dominican Order keep us together as Dominicans. Without stories we should be deprived of remembrance, fail to find our own place in the present and remain without hope or expectation for the future.'

What appeals to him so much about the Dominican way of life comes out very clearly in 'Dominican Spirituality', the work of which these form the opening remarks.[5] It has a long and chequered history. As we saw, a first version was written as long ago as 1954 in connection with his work with the Dominican students of Louvain, but this was not actually published, having a limited circulation in a duplicated form. Twenty years later a revised version was given as a lecture to Dominican sisters, and it has at last found its way into print in *God among Us*, the collection of articles and sermons published in 1983.

Even here, he makes it quite clear that he is no Dominican 'fundamentalist', and that such a position is quite wrong. Quoting Vatican II's Decree on the Renewal of Religious Life, he points out that to follow Jesus is the supreme norm of any form of religious life and that therefore being a Dominican is not a matter of following Dominic but above all of following Jesus. And because since the time of Dominic it has become possible to have a fuller – and more complex – understanding of Jesus, e.g. through modern biblical criticism or through the nature of devotional experience in the modern world, modern Dominican emphases may well be different from those of Dominic and his first followers. The Christian life is always opening up new possibilities, for which even Dominic himself did not know the all-embracing 'Open Sesame'. Moreover, the story of any Order must be seen in a wider context, as part of the story of the church, and that means that Dominican spirituality cannot be a matter of cultivating a private little garden.

Nevertheless, when all this has been said, the original inspiration of the Order still has a valid role to play. However, there can be no appealing to this inspiration as an authority by simply telling stories about the past. Dominican spirituality has to be a living reality today, handed on by members of the Order who reshape it in the light of contemporary conditions in the world and in the church. Unless that happens, the Order will indeed turn into a community of old people, and no new members will come to join it. ' "Spirituality" is not spirituality so long as it is only described, perhaps in an assertive or authoritarian tone. It is spirituality to the degree that it is realized in practice – as a completely new rendering of an older Dominican strain."[6]

When he goes on to define the nature of Dominican spirituality, Schillebeeck makes a great deal of use of the term 'cross-grained': a characteristic of the Order is as it were to weave a thread across the fabric of the ongoing history of the church. That is evident from the story that he tells.

It begins with Domingo de Guzman (1170-1221), the Augustinian canon of Osma, who took a group of helpers with him to the diocese of Toulouse, in southern France, to provide pastoral care in a difficult situation. A great many lay people had joined religious movements in which preaching the gospel was combined with a life of poverty in accordance with the precepts of Jesus; these movements were also often anti-clerical. Many abuses on the part of the clergy had raised the question whether Christian preaching had to be authorized by the church. Was not preaching combined with life in accordance with the gospel sufficient authentication in itself? The problem was complicated by the fact that these movements were strongly influenced by the Cathari coming in from Eastern Europe, who regarded the body and anything connected with it as evil; only the soul had been created by God. This led to extreme forms of behaviour. Like others, Dominic was concerned to gain the gospel movements for the church: his aim was to 'live like the heretics' but 'teach like the church'. His answer was to combine in the same community preaching authenticated by Pope or bishop with life in accordance with the gospel, and in this way the Order of Preachers was born.

The formation of the new Order brought considerable changes, despite the fact that it drew on features of the rules of already existing foundations for its constitutions. That the preachers were itinerant meant that they lacked the economic stability of the old established communities; their travelling also altered the nature of the contemplative element in their life. And their form of government was democratic, rather than government in monarchical fashion from above. All this amounted to an inbuilt tension between the religious values of the past and the religious promise of the future, and it is this that Schillebeeckx sees as the special characteristic of the Order. Not that this tension exists as an end in itself; it is a necessary element in the quest for truth, which for Dominic was an essential.

Schillebeeckx delights in pointing out the changes which this tension could produce. We have already seen how Albert and Thomas Aquinas championed the teaching of Aristotle and how Albert criticized those in the Order who called down anathemas on things they did not understand. In fact the Constitutions dating from the year of Dominic's death expressly forbade the study of pagan writers and philosophers (i.e. Aristotle and Arabic philosophy), 'much less the secular sciences'. Yet Albert and Thomas won the day to such a degree that in due course centres were actually built for the study of Arabic.

If the cross-thread in the Dominican history breaks, Schillebeeckx fears that Dominican spirituality will fade; he regrets the way in which Thomas Aquinas ceased to be a pointer towards the future and turned into an authority of the past to whom reference was to be made. He sees the greatest moments in the Dominican story as being the times when history becomes anti-history, and quotes the names of famous Dominicans by way of illustration. After Dominic, Albert and Thomas there is Girolamo Savonarola (1452-1498), who denounced the immorality of the clergy and people of Florence and proposed a reform of the city's government, eventually to be excommunicated by the Pope and hanged in the market place of Florence by its people; Meister Eckhardt (c.1260-1327), the great German mystic who was tried for heresy in Cologne and died during the appeal proceedings to the Pope; Bartolome de las Casas (1474-1566), who championed the Indians of the Caribbean and Latin America against their exploitation by the Spanish settlers; Henri Dominique Lacordaire (1802-1861), who re-established the Order in France after the Revolution; Marie-Joseph Lagrange

(1855-1938), who founded the Ecole Biblique in Jerusalem and was a pioneer in Catholic biblical criticism; Marie-Dominique Chenu (b.1895), whom we have already seen as a great influence on Schillebeeckx's thought,[7] and Yves Congar (b.1905), the doyen ecumenist. At the same time he notes that in weaving the cross-thread Dominicans have often got into trouble with the authorities. Although he is well aware of the contribution made by anonymous Dominicans quietly living out the Dominican religious life, he feels that 'it only becomes clear what is typically Dominican when Dominicans sometimes, following the example of Dominic, reshape the old and combine it with the dynamism of constantly new and different forms. If this does not happen at regular intervals the Dominican concern for truth may be thwarted and have to be represented elsewhere. Failures in the past, like the Inquisition, and the time when Dominicans shut up St Ignatius Loyola in their cellars, are to be seen as lessons which the Order must learn for the future.

When he talks about the tension inherent in Dominican spirituality, Schillebeeckx is fond of using two terms from Lacordaire, *présence au monde, la grâce d'entendre ce siècle*, and *présence à Dieu*. In the modern world, the former can mean that the priest or religious has to live among others, especially workers, not speaking openly of God or the church but being there in the hope that the Christian life-style may lead people to sense a deeper mystery, and raising the religious question simply by a way of life. *Présence à Dieu*, being in the presence of God, may perhaps, he feels, be possible only through this *présence au monde*, as it is shown in the signs of the time (again we see here the influence of his inspiration, Chenu). As far as the Order is concerned, this confirms the need for structures which do not hem its members in but are democratic and flexible, and through which it is possible for Dominicans to accept and integrate new stories which go against the grain. Schillebeeckx points out that the Dominicans never had their Constitutions approved by the Pope, so that they themselves were free to adapt them to new circumstances.

The trend introduced by Albertus Magnus is also a fundamental element in Dominican spirituality, namely what Schillebeeckx calls 'the principle of secularization'. Whereas the first Dominicans were anti-philosophical, after a good deal of agonizing the introduction of 'natural sources' was accepted. In other words, value was seen in first coming to know things (objects, inter-personal relationships, society) in their intrinsic characteristics and structures rather than prematurely defining their relationship to God. This has proved an enormous strength in the modern world.

That such an attitude won through was due, not least, to the 'principle of dispensation', an element in Dominican spirituality which Schillebeeckx particularly prizes. The principle was a completely new discovery for the Middle Ages. What it amounts to is allowing the individual freedom to pursue his personal calling within the Dominican community, bearing in mind the purpose of the Order. Because it amounts to a legitimation of non-conformity, it can be an extremely dangerous principle, but Dominic preferred to take the risk. In a contemporary setting it means that experimental spirituality is quite in order, even if it causes offence to those accustomed to a more 'established' pattern.

'No theologian, canon lawyer, professional psychologist or sociologist,' he therefore concludes, 'can work out at his study desk or in his armchair what we must do now. This must be tried by way of concrete experiment, by charismatically inspired religious, bearing in mind the sometimes dangerously cross-grained element – the golden thread – in our Dominican story. In so doing it will adopt, with due criticism, the successful attempts in the context of our past, gratefully rethinking them and making them fruitful in the context of the new programme.'[8]

And then comes a moving personal conclusion which brings us back to the problems facing the Order and the priesthood today:

All of us who are Dominicans today, men and women, are the only ones who can give it a new twist so that the story flourishes again (not as a stunt or a sensation but as an authentic Dominican family story), so that others in turn will join the Dominican storytelling community and continue to hand the story on. Here we may also happily pass on the folklore which each Order has alongside its own great story: that simply points to the fact that the great Dominican family story is made up of, and told by, ordinary, very human, people, though they transcend themselves through the strength of God's unmerited and loving grace. However, it would be fatal for the Dominican family story if this greater story eventually became narrrower and was reduced to the story of the folklore of Dominican houses. I am aware that I have said a great deal and very little. That is perhaps the most appropriate thing for the chapter which we are all adding, here and now, to the story of a great family tradition. I hope that it will become a serial which lasts longer than the stories which have entranced the whole world on television, but which have not in any way renewed the face of the earth: Peyton Place, the Forsyte Saga or Dallas. May the Dominican story be a parable which in an unspoken, but compelling, way ends with the words of Jesus: 'Go and do likewise'.[9]

Except that that is not the end of Schillebeeckx's account. The story so far has been one of male religious; and that is only the half of it. Even before Dominic was thinking of a Dominican Order, he had founded a convent, at Prouille, also with the intention of winning over members of the new gospel movements into the church. Others followed, but by the end of Dominic's life there was great opposition from the male side of the Order: Dominicans had enough to do without having to care for the sisters. There followed a prolonged struggle, the Pope and the sisters versus the rest of the Dominicans. Only the passage of time and a good deal of diplomacy led to a solution, in which the sisters won their case. Here, Schillebeeckx implies, there is an implicit pointer towards the case for women's liberation in the religious Orders as in the world outside; and that inevitably leads into the whole question of political theology, the subject of the next chapter.

Those who have come to this chapter expecting to find some insights into Schillebeeckx's spiritual life or to discover aspects resembling the best of Catholic devotional material in his work will have been disappointed. As we have already seen,[10] although when pressed in an interview, he will refer to his trust in God, his conversation with God, his faith and his freedom from anxiety, he is not one to wear his heart on his sleeve. His most 'devotional' book is probably his 1954 study of Mary, and that is a very early work indeed. But that does not make him someone for whom spirituality is incidental. Rather, his whole approach necessitates a complete revision of many definitions of spirituality, and if in addition to them there are other things that are left unsaid, it is good that one should not put everything into print or before the public gaze, but keep some of them for where they belong, in that private area where the individual, in the company of the church, comes face to face with God.

8

Political Theology

We saw in the previous chapter that Schillebeeckx has a firm belief that there will always be those who will keep the flame of the gospel alive with the oil of their lives. At the end of the sermon which he preached on the anniversaries of the profession and ordination of some of his fellow Dominicans, he introduces, from a book by L. Bessières, *Les acrobates de Dieu*, a grim yet moving illustration of what he has in mind.

> In 1974, in an indescribably terrifying place where hundreds of people had been shut up for months by the victors in a dictatorial coup d'état, a prisoner suddenly began to play his guitar. He sang of the stubborn hope of an enslaved people. A guard came past and with a blow of his sabre struck off the singer's hand. The song stopped. But then all the prisoners went on with it, though they were poor and wavering shadows. At the risk of execution they took up the thread of the song of the singer who was bleeding to death. This is the sharp and acid brilliance of enslaved people who at the risk of their lives sing in a boundless way, the way, of the real measure of our astonishing humanity.[1]

This illustration gives us a drastic reminder of the state of countless millions in the Third World, living under oppressive regimes, being imprisoned, tortured and executed – and even where their condition is not quite as bad as that, suffering from famine and all the ills of poverty, exploited by the rich West, which makes up a much smaller proportion of the world's population. If the gospel of the kingdom of God is for the poor, the insignificant and the oppressed, then it is for these people, and if for them salvation is to be anything worthy of the name, as we have seen, then that salvation must include a physical improvement in their lives, and that is bound to require political action. And that bring us to the question of political theology, which, since the series of writings which begin with *Jesus*, can be seen to be the ultimate character of Schillebeeckx's own theology.

In fact he does not believe that the great churches of the West, plagued as they are by domestic questions, can ever be an instrument for the liberation of the poor. Thus his own personal view is that the future of the church no longer lies in Europe or North America, but in Latin America and Africa. It is not that there is no concern with political theology and liberation among Christians of Western Europe and America. The Western world has its liberation theologians, and – as we have seen – alternative communities in which people attempt to come to a deeper and more existential criticism of the church and society as it is. But from the perspective of Latin America all this seems to be no more than flirting with political theology. Some of the most prominent European political theologians, Schillebeeckx argues, do not really analyse the social structures within which we live and what they write smacks too much of the study. Their work doesn't cost enough. And even where there are basic communities, harsh though it may seem, it has to be pointed out that those most involved in them come from the middle classes.

Those who feel that they are being got at with this criticism might well want to ask how Schillebeeckx differs from them. What is there about him and his approach which makes him in any way superior? He takes the point. To be consistent, he remarked in an interview before his retirement, he should really resign his professorial chair and go to live elsewere. But he could hardly say that he lived a bourgeois life, even if it was hard to light any flame for a younger generation from his present surroundings. However, his life was not yet over, and he might do something in his retirement. (On this occasion he also made the point, relevant to political theology, that the young often fall short of what the old have dreamed and those over the age of sixty-five may prove to have more to say than the middle generation.)[2]

In the West, Schillebeeckx's criticism goes on, what is called for most of all is structural change. If we find the situation in much of the Third World horrific, then we also have to realize that the

Western world is to blame for it. But that does not mean that people should therefore be seized by a sense of corporate guilt; that doesn't lead anywhere. As we have come to expect from his approach, he calls for a combination of thought and action. We need to realize just how wrong Western structures and the capitalist means of production are. This involves coming to terms with Marxist thought, since all our economies are bourgeois economies, which have not only brought about our current Western way of life but have also influenced the pattern of our thinking to a much greater degree than we ever recognize.

Take, for instance, Schillebeeckx argues, the accepted way of interpreting the Bible in our Western churches. What we assume to be an understanding of the teaching of Jesus can be compromised by the hidden influence of assumptions drawn from our social background which determine the range of what we feel to be asked of us. That becomes quite plain if we look at the way in which commentators on the Bible from a Latin American background make it seem to be quite a different book from the Bible to which we have grown accustomed. Schillebeeckx can cite Fernando Belo, a pioneer of 'materialist exegesis' with his *A Materialist Interpretation of the Gospel of Mark*,[3] which moves beyond the position taken by most New Testament scholars during this century of considering only the teaching of Jesus in the context of the church, to considering how the New Testament church was also affected by the social and economic conditions of the time. (Those unfamiliar with Belo's book, which has only just been translated into English after a long interval, will find a similar approach in Miranda's *Marx and the Bible*,[4] applied over a wider canvas.) However, like all new developments, this one goes to extremes. It is perverse, Schillebeeckx rightly points out, to want to dismiss as bourgeois all previous exegesis from the past two thousand years and too narrow to apply materialist exegesis to every passage of the Bible. Belo ends up by giving, not a Marxist reading of Mark, but a Marcan reading of Marx, repeating what Marx said about dialectical materialism and then filling it with texts from Mark.[5] By a kind of fundamentalist approach, and perhaps because of the particular circumstances in which it is produced, without the library facilities in which other New Testament interpretations so often rely, much writing in this vein concentrates overmuch on the text of the New Testament. For example, neglecting all the economic studies of the time that have been produced, like Rostovtzeff's three-volume *Social and Economic History of the Hellenistic World*, written as long ago as the time of the Second World War,[6] it tries to reconstruct the social situation of the time from the New Testament instead of using information from elsewhere. And such attempts are hazardous, because the New Testament rarely provides the kind of material being looked for.

However, that does not mean that there is no basis for political theology in the New Testament. Ever since Reimarus argued in the eighteenth century that Jesus was concerned with an earthly kingdom which was later wrongly transformed into a heavenly one, there have been scholars who have attempted to make a direct link between Jesus and the need for Christians to be involved in political action. In particular, over the last decade or so, as the image of 'Jesus the liberator' has become more popular, numerous studies have appeared with such titles as *Jesus and the Revolutionaries of his Time* or *Was Jesus a Revolutionist?*[7] However, Schillebeeckx gives short shrift to anyone who attempts to draw conclusions too hastily from the New Testament. He points out that those Christians who favour liberation theology or political theology or are generally critical of society tend to call the biblical Christ political, whereas churches who want to adopt an apolitical or even neutral attitude find arguments in the New Testament for attributing an apolitical attitude to Jesus. In each case they put their questions to the Bible in search of an answer that they want, without analysing historical conditions. This Schillebeeckx rightly sees as a kind of fundamentalism. In any circumstances it is wrong to use the question 'Was Jesus a Zealot?' to answer the question what our attitude should be to the problems of institutions and structures.

The authors of the two studies mentioned above, the New Testament scholars Oscar Cullmann and Martin Hengel, were in fact concerned to show that Jesus was not a revolutionary. But why, Schillebeeckx asks? Even if he were not, that does not mean that we should not be revolutionaries now! And he goes on to point out that while they may be right in arguing that on the basis of New Testament evidence Jesus was an apolitical figure it should not be forgotten that the New Testament had an apologetic interest in depicting Jesus as apolitical. It removed from the life of Jesus all those elements which might prove unacceptable to the Romans to avoid a persecution of the church; only in Revelation is he seen as the great fighter against unjust powers. Which goes to show that in using the New Testament, as we have learnt elsewhere, it is important to understand the historical attitudes of the communities whose witness it contains.[8]

While we may not argue directly in this way from Jesus' supposed political attitude to present day situations, we can see that his view of the kingdom of God in which there would be no master-servant relationships is extremely significant for politics. One text to which Schillebeeckx attaches great importance is Luke 22.25-27: 'Jesus said to them: "The kings of the Gentiles exercise lordship over them; and those in authority over them are called benefactors. But not so with you; rather let the greatest among you become as the youngest, and the leader was one who serves. For which is the greater, one who sits at table or one who serves? Is it not the one who sits at table? But I am among you as one who serves." ' According to this, and to Jesus' preaching of the kingdom of God it is quite clear that inward change, conversion, goes hand in hand with a change in social structures and relationships. Because of their limited possibilities the first Christians could attempt to realize this only within their own communities, but Jesus' message clearly implies that *all* relationships must be renewed, including those on a political level. That means that we have to live and work for new conditions, drawing our own conclusions from the fact of the dawn of the kingdom of God.[9]

If necessary, Schillebeeckx argues, that may mean using force. In some instances such violence may be done to groups that they find themselves with their backs to the wall. The use of force here in self-defence is very different from the active use of power by dictatorships. Violence is always an evil, but sometimes it may be necessary to choose the lesser evil because passiveness and inactivity simply mean that oppressive structures go on.

Another New Testament passage which is extremely important to Schillebeeckx is Jesus' parable of the sheep and the goats in Matthew 25, which introduces a new dimension into the discussion. The parable, Schillebeeckx points out in a moving sermon on it,[10] represents a projection by Matthew of what Jesus said and did as a standard for the last judgment. Matthew knows that in Jesus the divinity of God appeared as the achievement of greater humanity between fellow human beings, as exemplified by giving a glass of water from a precious store to thirsty people in the searing heat of the desert. The parable, he observes, is almost atheistic seeing that the name of God is mentioned only in it when the judgment is over. It does not matter whether we have praised God liturgically as King of the universe or have supported the church and its organization; the one question asked in the judgment is whether we have personally or structurally helped those in need, and particularly the lowly and the oppressed.

At first sight there seems to be nothing specifically Christian about Matthew's story, and in fact if we look at other literature from the same period we find exactly the same imagery used to describe humane treatment. However, what is different in Matthew is the identification of the judge making the judgment with the person in need. 'You have done this to *me*.' By means of this identification Matthew indicates that it is the oppressed of the world who will judge us by the standard of the suffering which has been inflicted on them. Hence the primacy of the call to relieve suffering as a way of realizing the kingdom of God.

Discussing the same passage in an interview Schillebeeckx went even further. On the basis of what Jesus says there, in the light of a Christian interpretation there is no essential difference, say between the death of Martin Luther King and that of a communist guerrilla fighter in El Salvador who has no direct links with Christianity.[11] In giving their lives for the liberation of mankind both are fulfilling the criteria laid down by Jesus. He seems even to go so far as to say that Jesus' death is to be identified with the death of anyone who gives his life in a popular movement for liberation. He accepts the interviewer's suggestion that Jesus is messiah along with all the others who have seen God's cause as man's cause whether they realize it or not, though to balance that it has also to be said that we would not have known this had Jesus not shown it to us first.

The seriousness with which Schillebeeckx takes the universalist dimension of this parable is also evident from his criticism of some forms of liberation theology which in his view fall short of it. He feels that its full dimensions have not been realized, for example, in the Latin-American liberation theologian Gustavo Gutierrez's pioneering study *Theology of Liberation*.[12] Gutierrez, he argues, while being in favour of liberation as praiseworthy human action, sees divine grace as a factor in addition to it. That, he claims, is being too dualistic. Where liberation takes place, grace is to be found actually *in* the process of liberation. For the New Testament, he points out, grace is not set over against nature or creation, like the natural and the supernatural in later scholastic theology, but over against sin and helplessness. It is not a metaphysical concept but an experience of reality which is called 'grace' when described from the perspective of faith.

In the New Testament, grace – and again it should not be forgotten that the original Dutch title of *Christ* included the word, so that it plays a large part in the discussion – is closely connected with liberation, and Schillebeeckx explores its many dimensions in one of those lists of variant significances of which he is so fond. This one has as many as sixteen elements:

1. Grace is connected with salvation and redemption.
2. Grace means being freed from forms of servitude and slavery
3. Grace is redemption, i.e. being freed through purchase or for a ransom.
4. Grace is reconciliation after a dispute.
5. Grace is satisfaction and making good.
6. Grace is the expiation of sins.
7. Grace is the forgiveness of sins.
8. Grace is justification and sanctification.
9. Grace is having the support of Jesus as advocate before the heavenly Father.
10. Grace is being redeemed for community.
11. Grace is being freed for brotherly love.
12. Grace is being freed for freedom.
13. Grace is the renewal of man and the world.
14. Grace is life in fullness.
15. Grace is victory over demonic powers.
16. Grace leads to prayer and celebration.

These specific ideas of grace, which is also salvation in God through Jesus and the fulfilment of our humanity, indicate – Schillebeeckx concludes, that New Testament Christianity is not content with generalities and vagueness, or cries of 'We are free'. It adds specific detail, by defining what Christians feel themselves to be freed from and for what they know themselves to be free. It is also evident that despite the objective foundation of their hope, the life, death and resurrection of Jesus, Christians still have to bring about liberation in the dimension of history: 'That it is concerned with more than an appeal to good will and co-humanity is shown by the fact that powers of slavery are at work *in* our world which (in accordance with the world view of the time) are identified with the world of heavenly demons.'[13] And Schillebeeckx refers to the powers of darkness of Ephesians 6.12.

It should be evident by now how for Schillebeeckx, political theology is not the superficial politicizing of the gospel which can be found with other writers who express their commitment with greater vehemence and less reflection. Specific circumstances of oppression and injustice in the modern world lead him deep into the New Testament and to the message of Jesus, and steeping himself in the world of first-century Christianity deepens his understanding of what is required of Christians today. There could hardly be a better practical instance of the principle of correlation which Schillebeeckx argues is the approach that we should adopt.

Nor does he ever divorce political theology from the prayer and worship of the church. It is not enough, he stresses, to want to politicize the Christian community and to minimalize liturgy, prayer and contemplation. The church of Christ is a church of mysticism and a church of liberation. Indeed, if we go back to the beginnings of the three great monotheistic religions, Judaism, Christianity and Islam, we find that while each is profoundly concerned with this world, their inspiration is a very central mystical experience. For the Jews, Moses, the political leader who brought his people liberation was the mystic who spoke with God face to face, as a man speaks with his friend. Mohammed had nocturnal encounters with angels of Allah who communicated the Qu'ran to him straight from heaven. And with Jesus, the heart of his whole mission on behalf of the poor and the oppressed was his mystical experience of God as Abba, Father. 'In Jesus, mysticism and the liberation of the world came from one and the same source: his experience of contrast between the living God and the history of human suffering.'[14]

A church concerned with liberation and the improvement of the world which has no mysticism is only half a church, for not only is the God's kingdom the liberating source of all liberation, but in addition we have to overcome subtle forms and causes of oppression the existence of which cannot be discovered without mysticism and the experience of God. Schillebeeckx has much that is positive to say about the contribution that Eastern religions can make to Western spirituality in this dimension. However, it is interesting that he is fully aware of the way in which emphasis on mysticism could become dangerous. Not, he stresses, because of the influence of Eastern mysticism itself, but because of the misuse that Western society and its controlling forces could make of this mystical revival. He indicates quite specifically what he has in mind in this passage:

In America, many meditation centres receive outside financial support, not so much because people want to subsidize a praise-worthy cultural phenomenon but often on the basis of the cool calculation that the more young people drop out of society as contemplatives, the less revolutionary potential will remain to offer fierce criticism of the social structures and react violently with calls for change. The very thing that many contemplatives challenge, our society bent on success and achieved through vicious competition, is confirmed and safeguarded by their own marginalization. This society does not look for better things; if it did, it would not be disturbed by critical elements.[15]

We have moved some way from Schillebeeckx's concern for Christianity and justice in the Third World and particularly in Latin America. However, these days that concern is seldom far from his thoughts in whatever he may be speaking or writing about. There could hardly be a clearer indication of this than a passage, not by him, in the last chapter of *Ministry*.

The preface to *Ministry* is dated 10 August 1980; on 5 July of that year the Dutch journal *NRC Handelsblad* published a letter sent in the name of thousands of priests from Latin America to Pope John Paul II on the occasion of his visit to Brazil. Schillebeeckx simply inserted that letter into his book with the briefest of introductions, obviously seeing a closer connection between its contents and the rest of *Ministry* than might be immediately obvious to a less committed reader.

Here is some of what the letter says; those who find Schillebeeckx's views on the subject of political theology extreme may find that it helps them to understand why he feels as he does.

The first colonists found the original inhabitants of this land 'primitive' and 'uncared for'. That was sufficient justification for one of the most blatant cases of genocide in human history. The indigenous population was decimated and oppressed in the name of Jesus Christ. His cross, the symbol of redemption, took the form of the sword of the conqueror which was blessed by all but the good pastors of their church. This dishonouring of the gospel and the involvement of the church with the colonists and their system have been a source of serious ambiguities in the faith which still persist even now.

We believe that the time has come for the Catholic Church to confess its sins. It should acknowledge that it too was involved in Spanish and Portuguese colonization. We think that it must engage in self-criticism, which is without doubt healthy, especially for itself. . .

We, servants of Christ, incarnate in the story of the 'poor of Yahweh', are certain that he is also alive on our continent and eats bread with the hungry and thirsts for righteousness on behalf of those of our people who live in prisons and suffer torture and death in the fields. He is also present in the thousands of men, women and children who suffer from malnutrition. Therefore we stand for true liberation and fight alongside the people in the name of this Jesus Christ.

Millions of brothers have gone before us in the same fight. Like them, we too are aware of the risks that we run and of the responsibility that we are taking upon ourselves. What Christ could not have suffered we are willing to suffer for him, for his body the church, and as a proclamation of his resurrection. The proof of that lies with those who, in total surrender, have paid for this with their own lives. Along with non-believing *companeros*, bishops too have fallen in the fight; and many sisters and priests, and thousands of Christians. . .

Illuminated by the example of this 'greatest love' of those who 'offered their life for their friends', and starting from the experiences of our oppressed and murdered brothers who keep demanding justice, we stress that our participation in this process is a biblical command and that we must therefore continue it. . .

We think that to 'choose for the poor' in Latin America is a political choice. That is the way in which it is understood by many

Christians, and despite all the risks, we are prepared to keep our promise to the end. There must be an end to vagueness and neutral attitudes. . .

We want to end with the words of our Bishop Martin Oscar Arnulfo Romero: 'The cry of this people for liberation is a cry which goes up to God and which nothing and no one can keep back.'[16]

While Schillebeeckx's main concern for political theology grew out of his acquaintance with the Latin American churches and the problems there, and the Latin American situation colours much of what he say, political theology includes one issue which arises, if at all, in a different form in Latin America because of the social conditions there and which is most prominent in the countries of the Western world.

Translating books by Schillebeeckx, one is made very aware of his concern not to use sexist language. Although English is not his native tongue, conversations particularly in America have made him very conscious that words which in European continental languages are accepted as being of common gender, in England and America can be understood as endorsing male supremacy. He reads through the English versions of his books, and any term that might seem to be exclusively male is rigorously excluded, even if the resultant rendering is rather more clumsy.

This awareness of language is a new development from a decade ago, as indeed is the impact of 'women's lib', and is one indication of the way in which slight progress is being made, at least in some limited areas. Schillebeeckx has acknowledged that the appearance of new books has made him constantly aware of the need to think in feminist terms (though he would reject superficial attempts to remedy the situation by suggesting that we should talk about God as 'she' and 'mother'). The important thing is not so much to change culturally conditioned words in the Bible as to provide real emancipation in our society for women. For example, it has to be remembered that all the great religions of the world derive from agricultural backgrounds. To transform these religions so that they reflect the needs and responses of the modern world, in which women enjoy a quite different degree of freedom, requires a great deal of thought and new forms of praxis.

Feminist theology, Schillebeeckx points out, has discovered a basic fault in Western theology which goes back as far as the time of Augustine.[17] It has stressed that the chief human sin is that of arrogance, a preoccupation with self-affirmation. That is all very well for those who are already in a position of domination, as a reminder not to go beyond fulfilling under God the proper responsibilities of their position. When applied by men to women within sexist and patriarchal structures, it induces oppression and even humiliation, and introduces perverted ideas of pride and self-sacrifice. The church's dominant doctrines of sin and grace have encouraged women to be passive and to abase themselves. Feminist theologians have come to see that an authentic doctrine of grace and sin must include the liberating freedom of responsible self-affirmation with and for others.

He identifies two tendencies in feminist theology. On the one hand there are those who are concerned to expose all elements in Christian theological thinking which discriminate against women. This trend, which is dominant above all in America, is more concerned with a change of mentality within the church. Its overriding aim is that there should be a new interpretation of the Bible and the tradition of the church, above all of those sayings of the Church Fathers which are hostile to women. On the other hand, particularly in Europe, there is a trend which is oriented much more on a concern for the place of women in society - including their place in the church. This concern has a much greater sociological orientation and when introduced into theology makes theology only a repetition of what critical sociologists have been saying. It is weaker when tackling the question of the way in which the forms in which revelation has come to us must change and even be rewritten if discrimination against women is to cease.

Feminist theology, he realizes, is still in the making, and a good deal of its task must at present consist in opening male eyes to things which at present they are unable to see. To much of what feminist theologians say males can only retort, 'You're right'. But if they are prepared to do that the sensitivity of theologians and the way in which they build up their systems will change to such a degree that theology takes on quite a different form.

In connection with feminist theology, as indeed in connection with political theology, there is still a great deal to be said and even more to be done. So Schillebeeckx has indicated that further discussion on these subjects will occupy a good deal of the third volume of his planned great trilogy, and that still lies in the future. However, that does not mean that one can simply note what he says and wait. For it should be evident by now that all his theology is in one sense or another political theology, and calls for a response and effective action now.

9

'A Brief Hermeneutical Intermezzo'

The title of this chapter comes from Schillebeeckx himself; he uses it to describe the half-dozen pages in *Ministry* which precede the survey of the 1971 Synod of Bishops, the letter of the Latin American priests and the prospect on the future with which the book ends.[1] His aim there is to forestall possible objections to what he is about to say, in particular the charge that the whole of the historical survey which we considered in Chapter 7 has been written with an eye to his final conclusions. Since precisely the same charge was made against his *Jesus*, as we have already seen, this is clearly a sensitive point and one on which he rightly feels that he is often misunderstood.

His answer to the question whether he has not read the history of the development of ministry with an eye to the present is, to begin with, a disarming 'Of course'. But that does not mean that he meekly yields to the accusation. There is a good deal more to be said. The only way in which history *can* be read, he points out, is in the light of our own contemporary questions and concerns. Even the person who claims to read ancient documents in a 'neutral' way cannot think away his or her own present; they are simply unaware of their own hidden interests. The key question is whether one allows these interests to be put to the test by history.

If we are sufficiently interested in a book, like the Bible, written two thousand years ago, we find ourselves engaged in a dialogue with it – the more technical term is that we are involved in a dialectical process with it – in such a way that we put our own questions to it and form our own answers to them from what we read. And that is the point at which we have to be careful. For we cannot read the past as though it had only just happened; it is not, Schillebeeckx points out, a computer from which stored information can constantly be drawn off afresh for our use. We need 'creative trust' in the texts we have from the past, allowing them to speak to us in their own terms without shouting them down with our own ideas. We have in common with writers and figures from the past that they are part of the human history in which we also share; we differ from them in that their world is not ours.

> The story began long before we start to take up its thread. Someone once said that the last thing that a fish (after achieving reflective awareness) would observe would be the water in which it lived: the 'today' of its own milieu. This is so familiar and obvious that it never strikes us. Thus everyone spontaneously reads the past through the prism of the present, his or her own present with its particular questions, presuppositions and hypotheses. To read a text critically and thus 'objectively' (in accordance with the material in question) is therefore also to be aware of all this; the uncritical readers of texts are those who want to read them 'unhistorically' and claim that they can exclude their own present in so doing.[2]

Today, he goes on, Christians have realized much more clearly that 'the will of God' is known to us only through history, and never directly. It comes to us through the medium of experiences in the world and in the church, and also through directives from the pastoral authority of the church. And because all of these are historically conditioned, it can be dangerous to talk of 'the will of God' if we forget that fact. Because the expressions of the will of God come through history, they too give rise to a dialectic. The Christian has to note the signs of the times, to pay heed to the suffering of human beings and the beginnings of new Christian communities, and then do what he or she feels called to do as a consequence. That can be 'doing the will of God'. And it can give rise to a conflict between obedience to the will of God as seen in the events of the world and obedience to the will of God as mediated through the authority of the church. This conflict is not caused by the will of God, but by the intermediaries which give different interpretations of it. And to end his 'Intermezzo' he quotes Thomas Aquinas to the effect that if a man's conscience has been tested in such a conflict, he (or she) can make his own decision; moreover, the conscientious person must do this 'even if he knows that as a result he can be excommunicated by the church'. To Aquinas' words Schillebeeckx adds his own: 'In my view this applies above all whenever the salvation and happiness of *others* are at stake (because one can always renounce one's own rights for the sake of something better).'[3]

With this discussion we are on the verge not only of a challenge to the church's traditional view of ministry but also of the whole question of hermeneutics.

Hermeneutics, a word from Greek and not unconnected with the Greek god Hermes is, in short, the science of interpretation and particularly the interpretation of texts. It is an area of theology which has received increasing attention over the past twenty or thirty years, and Schillebeeckx's concern with it goes back a long way. Hermeneutics first appears in Schillebeeckx's work in his book on marriage, written shortly after Vatican II.[4] However, it really began to seize his attention in 1966. In that year he had to give a new course at the University on hermeneutics, probably arising out of the new status of theology in the church after Vatican II. From that time onwards he gave at least one course on it each year, regularly revised (and sometimes more than one course), for the rest of his career. Going into the various aspects of the subject he found himself having to explore areas of knowledge of which he had previously been quite ignorant. His courses considered various German schools (Bultmann and the 'new hermeneutics' which came after him, Gadamer, Pannenberg, Habermas, Paul Ricoeur and structuralism, linguistic analysis and analytical philosophy ranging from Wittgenstein to Ian Ramsey. He also arranged interdisciplinary sessions, so that he gained knowledge of hermeneutical problems in areas other than theology.[5]

Virtually none of this work has been published; it can be seen as a long term preparation for the substantial book on hermeneutics which he plans for the future. However, all these studies have had their effect on his writing and, as we have already seen,[6] were a major factor in the circumstances leading up to his writing of *Jesus*. Schillebeeckx's discussion of the interpretation of the decrees of the Council of Trent which we looked at in Chapter 3 was a hermeneutical discussion, and we saw that *Jesus* begins with 'Questions of Method, Hermeneutics and Criteria'. In fact the book which immediately preceded *Jesus*, *The Understanding of Faith*, was exclusively devoted to hermeneutical questions, particularly in the light of Schillebeeckx's understanding of the contribution of the 'new critical theory' of Jürgen Habermas and the Frankfurt school.

However, it would be misleading just to single out individual passages from Schillebeeckx's later works to highlight his concern with hermeneutics. In fact, the whole of his theology, no matter what its immediate subject-matter may be, is hermeneutics, and throughout this book we have been examining that hermeneutics and have seen, without pausing to reflect on them, the principles which govern Schillebeeckx's interpretation of the Christian tradition. That makes it understandable that when he came to give his formal 'last lecture' on 11 February 1983, it should have been on hermeneutics.

The title of this last lecture, not yet translated into English, is an expansion of that of his earlier book on hermeneutics, 'The Theological Understanding of Faith in the Year 1983'.[7] And he quite explicitly introduces it as an account of how he himself does theology. Hearing those words his audience, though they were warned that they would hear no personal anecdotes, might not have expected quite what follows (and the structure of the lecture, with its disproportionate sub-divisions and rather strange system of numbering is vintage Schillebeeckx). To anyone unfamiliar with what Schillebeeckx has written and taught, this last lecture might seem like just one more technical study. But it really does say a good deal about his theology to those who know it, and as it is also a masterly statement about hermeneutics – it is as good as anything he has so far written on the subject – it forms an appropriate conclusion to our survey and leads well into a provisional assessment and to the theological works by Schillebeeckx which are still to come.

Theologians these days, Schillebeeckx points out, often ask the question 'What is theology?' (we have already seen their problem). But what they should really begin by asking is, 'Who is the theologian?' For whether he or she knows it or not, the thought of every theologian is coloured by his or her place in society, in the university, in the church, in a basic community or in everyday life. That is why theology today, in a pluralistic society, is itself so pluralistic: one has only to think of the difference between the liberation theology of Latin America and the dominant forms of theology in Europe or America. Like the fish in its water, one might say, academic theologians in Europe take for granted the objective, uncommitted approach of their discipline as if it were the only one possible, whereas they need to reflect on that, too, if their theology is not to turn into an ideology. And the same is equally true of those who claim to be simply handing down the traditions and dogmas of the church.

'Ideology' is an important term for Schillebeeckx. It is not, he argues when he comes to explain it, necessarily a pejorative term. Positively, an ideology is a collection of images, ideas and symbols created by a group or society in order to express its own identity. That positive understanding is the basic one; however, as time goes on the group or society can be manipulated and monopolized by elements whose influence leads to a pathological ideology, in which what was originally the expression of the group becomes something which takes on a pathological existence of its own and becomes an instrument of domination. Ideology then becomes a negative factor.[8]

Hermeneutics must always be critical of ideologies, of whatever kind (and some can be very insidious); it must unmask them, and in this process the theologian engaged in hermeneutics will find that theory always also involves praxis. Jesus' message of the kingdom of God was so integrated with his action that his preaching and his life-style interpreted each other while at the same time changing the situation of those with whom he came into contact.

These considerations frame the heart of Schillebeeckx's account of the nature of hermeneutics, a discussion of the relationship between two 'poles' which have to be held in tension in any hermeneutics, the tradition and the situation. Both these poles are extremely complex.

First, tradition. For all its ups and downs the tradition - and here Schillebeeckx speaks, though not exclusively, of the Christian tradition – can be seen as a cumulative disclosure of meaning and truth, and this is what those within it understand it to be. It also opens up a horizon of possible experience for us today and does so above all by telling stories. A good deal of interest is being currently expressed in narrative theology (and the footnote here lists a substantial number of works, largely from the English-speaking world), but that is hardly enough. As we saw right at the beginning of this book, for Schillebeeckx telling stories properly also involves being caught up in them. In connection with this he uses a phrase which we already came across in a narrower context in his discussion of Dominican spirituality: in the end what we are concerned with is the fusing of two stories, the story of the gospel tradition of faith and the story of our own personal and communal life. To illustrate what he means by this he comments on an incident from the Gospel of Luke which, to judge from his use of it in less formal situations, is a favourite of his:

> When Jesus saw tiny Zacchaeus, so small that he had to climb into a tree to watch Jesus pass by, he did not say to him 'God loves you' (like the modern fundamentalist posters in our crowded streets). Something rather different happened. Jesus went to his house and by eating and talking with him actually showed Zacchaeus that God loved him. By doing this he disclosed something which transcends our humanity. Zacchaeus abandoned his corrupt life and gave half his possessions to the poor.[9]

Tradition and its interpretation can therefore be summed up in another of Schillebeeckx's formidable phrases, 'the tradition of faith which discloses meaning with liberating force'. And that is why hermeneutics can never be a purely theoretical activity.

Situation, secondly, is an even more complex matter. In modern times Christians may be handing down their faith to new generations in the prosperous society of Western Europe, in non-Western societies now invaded by Western technology, in very different areas of the Third World like Latin America, Africa or South East Asia, or even to what has been referred to as 'le troisième homme', those in the West who have become alienated from their roots. So complex is this 'situation' that it cannot completely be analysed, and certainly no theory of it can be constructed. In such a complex world, within any particular area Christians may adopt very different attitudes which mean that their own situations can be even more varied. They may adopt to varying degrees, encourage, criticize or reject modern culture, both technology and the social structures within which they live. This means that Christian communities are likely to be very complex groups – and they are the ones whose reaction must be noted: Schillebeeckx never wearies of insisting that theology is a communal enterprise, and not the work of the individual theologian.

Hermeneutics, we have seen, is reflection on the interaction, the dialectic, between tradition and situation, which have the characteristics indicated above. Perhaps 'interaction between tradition and situation' may seem somewhat abstract and over-intellectual to those more used to thinking in terms of 'preaching the gospel', but for Schillebeeckx that is, rightly, the only accurate way of putting it. The gospel may be fundamentally transcendent and universal, but we only have it in the form given to it by particular cultures and ages: Jewish, Hellenistic, Carolingian, Celtic, Asiatic or whatever. There is no way of stripping off the skin and getting down to the essence of the gospel. And this combination of gospel and cultural conditioning applies not just to interpretations by churches in certain times and places, but to the very foundation documents of Christianity itself, the Bible, the creeds and the doctrinal statements of the church.

Given this, hermeneutics is not, then, a question of how to interpret Bible or doctrine in such a way as to be able to apply it to our contemporary situation. It is not as though one pole of the interrelationship, say the documents of the tradition, were a source to be drawn on to irrigate the other, our present situation; the situation is not simply the bed through which the stream of tradition runs. What we have is the encounter of different cultural forms of the same understanding of faith and the different life-styles that go with them. God is active and reveals himself creatively *in* the interaction comprised by this encounter.

Such a position contrasts markedly with other ideas of how Christian faith is arrived at in the modern world. It stands between the extremes of, on the one hand, the stress on a positivism of revelation (like Barth and Bultmann's 'theology of the Word') or tradition (like the traditional understanding of the teaching of the Roman Catholic Church) in which one of the two 'poles' is normative, or, on the other hand, the nineteenth-century liberal model in which the other has absolute authority. It resembles most closely that represented by a great English theologian, Leonard Hodgson, who concerned himself with these matters long before 'hermeneutics' became a theologically fashionable word (interestingly, Schillebeeckx never seems to refer to him in any of his footnotes) whose famous question, posed years ahead of its time, has influenced much contemporary English theology: 'What must the truth be now if people who thought as they did put it like that?'[10] Hodgson's question has sometimes been thought to imply that 'the truth' is something like a constant nucleus encapsulated within ever-changing forms, but like Schillebeeckx, he is well aware of the complications, and a passage from his last book serves as a lucid comment on Schillebeeckx's position, though it was written almost twenty years ago:

> The New Testament shows its writers trying to make head or tail of what had happened on the basis of their Jewish understanding of God and the universe. So far from having given us a full and final explanation of the meaning of our faith they were taking the first steps towards its discovery, initiating a process which under the guidance of the Holy Spirit has been continuing ever since and is still going on . . . we have to take into account how the understanding of it by the New Testament Christians has been deepened and enriched in the experience of their successors and is still being deepened and enriched by our experience of life in the world today.[11]

Schillebeeckx never loses the sense of exploration, of discovery, mentioned by Hodgson; he is fond of contrasting what we can see of the past, after the event, with our view of the present while we are in the thick of things. Without the benefit of hindsight contemporary theologians may as well fail as succeed, may distort the tradition as well as illuminate it.

And that brings us to the next question. It is not enough to talk simply of 'interaction between tradition and situation' as if this were a natural process. The term denotes an activity of church communities and theologians which is carried on by human beings, men and women, with their own distinctive concerns and even personalities. And because they are in the thick of things, criteria are necessary. So: how do we know that a particular theological insight leading to particular praxis is right or wrong? What are the standards for theology if they cannot, as the position already outlined indicates, be a simple reference to the gospel or the dogma of the church?

At an earlier stage in his writing, in *The Understanding of Faith*, when one of his prime concerns was the relevance of Anglo-Saxon analytical philosophy, Schillebeeckx replied to this question with a reference to John Hick's notion of 'eschatological verification'.[12] From the purely theological point of view, orthodoxy cannot be verified; this verification can only be an eschatological event, i.e. we shall have to wait until the end of the journey. But, he continued, the theologian who wants to write a book about the Christian interpretation of reality cannot wait for that, and so he went on to present – as one of a group of inter-relating criteria, 'the criterion of the proportional norm'. At that time he defined this as 'a certain proportion in which subsequent expressions (in their different contexts) find themselves with regard to the intentionality of faith as inwardly determined by the mystery of Christ'.[13] In his last lecture, this idea of proportionality remains – and is indeed illustrated in diagrammatic form – but the obscurity and vagueness of the statement with which it is connected gives place to a much clearer account.

All theological positions must be capable of justification by reference to the tradition in which the theologian stands; in other words, theology is always a hermeneutic activity, connected with the past, though the methods it uses may be those of modern critical study. Moreover, all theological positions must be capable of justification by reference to the contemporary situation on the basis of a similar critical analysis. The theologian always has to look in two directions at once, but this looking in two directions belongs to one and the same activity. Because theologians do not look through 'innocent' eyes, they always have to examine their presuppositions critically. For example, in terms of the tradition in which they stand Catholic theologians will tend to have a positive view of the world and history, despite the ambivalence and horror of much of that history, whereas Protestants will tend to stress the brokenness and demonic character of our situation and take a more negative view. That means that Catholics need to remind themselves of the meaninglessness that is such a threat within human existence, while Protestants need to be aware of the history of divine revelation which is continually going on.

And so to the proportionality:

We never look the Christian identity straight in the face; it can never be determined once and for all. But that does not mean that it is quite arbitrary. The Christian identity, which is one and the same, is never a matter of direct likeness, but of proportional likeness: the unity is one in depth. Consequently we cannot understand 'the development of dogma' in the same way as the Scholastics or the Neo-Scholastics, or even in the same way as Newman, as the permanent explicitation of something which was always there implicitly, in a straight line from the Bible to the present day. The periodical kinks in the cultural understanding of reality rule out such a possibility. What we have is something rather different. It is a process of the constantly new 'inculturation' of the transcultural substance of the gospel, which does not exist and cannot be received apart from a specific cultural form. The consequences of this is that dogmas or confessions of faith are irreversible; we cannot pretend that they are not there. With a greater or lesser degree of success they have sought to express the mysteries of Jesus Christ and God within a particular social and cultural system of reference. On the other hand, in their cultural and historical forms they can become irrelevant to later genera-tions, because other generations express the same substance of faith in a different semantic field and by a different system of communications. Yet even irrelevant dogmas remain theologi-cally important. In a proportional way our present-day believing must always have the same character as the first Jewish interpret-ation of Jesus and the subsequent Hellenistic interpretation at the Council of Chalcedon.[14]

Interpretation, he concludes, makes new traditions, in creative trust. Christian identity consists in having the same fundamental view of God and man and the relationship between them and by virtue of that transcending the various culturally, geographically, socially or psychologically conditioned forms in which that view has to be expressed. The search for the right proportionality brings about the realization of the good news of the gospel.

The questioning goes on – in this instance not only by but of Schille-beeckx, for in this most difficult of all areas there are still many issues yet to be clarified, and much of what he says will be challenged not only by those who take a more traditional view of Christianity than he does but also by those who wonder whether having gone this far, the logic of things does not lead him far more deeply into the perplexing matter of cultural relativism. We shall have to wait for his large book on the subject.

One thing, though, is abundantly clear. This discussion of hermeneutics shows just how foolish the Vatican hierarchy is to attack Schillebeeckx in the way that it does, with what on any showing is an extraordinarily naive view of hermeneutics. As one commentator put it more than ten years ago, in the area in which Schillebeeckx is working, 'formal authority has ceased to function, in the sense that implicit convictions have to prove their value on the strength of their contents alone. In Schillebeeckx's thought this idea links up with his frequent emphasis on the need for dialogue and the increasing prominence he attributes to praxis over theory and orthopraxis over orthodoxy. But the relevance of these notions can only be seen properly when they are placed in the whole context of the synthesis Schillebeeckx is trying to get into focus.'[15]

The position is essentially the same as that which arose over the question of ministry. No statements from or actions by the church in this area can command respect if their basis is sheerly authoritarian. Just as the historical survey of the development of the ministry calls for a historical answer, so too does the whole of Schillebeeckx's hermeneutical approach – and that means the whole of his theology – calls for a convincing hermeneutical alternative if it is thought to be inadequate.

As things are, such an alternative seems hardly likely to issue from official circles, which by their very nature cannot be open to the stress on dialogue which has always been so much a part of Schillebeeckx's hermeneutical investigations. It is perhaps not too farfetched to compare this reluctance to engage in dialogue, to join in alongside the world in considering its own problems, with an earlier reluctance of representatives, many centuries ago, to look into a certain telescope. For in connection with the question of hermeneutics, which we have seen to be fundamental to the whole of Schillebeeckx's approach and his conclusions on a variety of issues, the official Roman Catholic position seems – proportionally – dangerously close to that of the church at the time of Galileo. The point at issue is rather more sophisticated than the relationship of the earth to the sun, but it is none the less just as intrinsically connected with the reality of our world and our existence.

10

Assessment – and the Future

In its time (and not always in mine) our 'turbulent little publishing house' of SCM Press has published some extremely controversial books as well as many of impeccable orthodoxy.[1] The controversial titles are inevitably the ones to attract the most attention, and these days, in the religious field, they are usually controversial because they question the deeply held affirmative convictions of a great many people, while at the same time seeming to bring liberation to a great many others. *Honest to God* (1963), *The Myth of God Incarnate* (1977) and *Taking Leave of God* (1980) are all books which have received a great deal of attention, not necessarily because of the details of what they say but because their essential subject-matter, the greatest question with which anyone can be concerned, namely the nature and destiny of human beings and whether there is a God within whose greater purposes and power that falls, has found an echo in people inside and outside the churches. Such books have had a double effect; they have proved helpful – often, it has to be acknowledged, in a somewhat bleak way (the author of the last-mentioned book talks of 'hyperborean faith')[2] – to some and have struck a deep chill into the heart of others. But by no stretch of the imagination can they really be called positive books. They are hardly full of great affirmations.

I never realized how deeply the chill had sunk in until a quite unexpected disclosure at a party. It was being given to celebrate the modernization of a large London bookshop. I had had a full day, and by the time I arrived many of the guests had already begun to leave. I knew some of those who were giving the party quite well, and found myself still talking with them at the stage when the glasses were being cleared away and everyone was ready to go home. One man, a devout Anglican layman who had worked extraordinarily hard to achieve the transformation we were celebrating and who had rightly been liberally supplied with wine by his colleagues as a tribute to his efforts, took me aside and asked me a question which he might not have got round to had it been the sober cold light of day. 'John,' he asked, in a slightly slurred voice, 'when are you going to publish something that gives us hope?'

The question rather took me aback at the time. I had been more inclined to see the liberating side of the demolition work that had been going on in theology and did not feel threatened by it. But I was now made to realize quite how much the constant chipping away at old fabric and foundations proved a worry to those without the technical knowledge to assess the new developments – which in less able writers, particularly in the 1960s, had led to statements which were totally negative (and wildly inaccurate) – or the perspective to see the positive results to which they could lead. It was quite a short conversation, but I have thought about it a great deal since.

Schillebeeckx's *Jesus* had not appeared at that time; had it done so, I would have immediately referred my friend to it, and above all to the biblical quotation from I Thessalonians, echoed in the prayer which for so many centuries has been used at Anglican funeral services, which appears on the dedication page: 'That you may not grieve as others do who have no hope.'

Schillebeeckx is above all the theologian who gives hope, and in fact he used that same quotation in another place, as the very last words of the very last lecture which he gave as a university professor.[3] He is not, like the German theologian Jürgen Moltmann, who made his name in that connection, a theologian of hope, in that he makes hope a theme of his discussion. It is simply there, a rock-steady confidence that comes from his belief and trust in the God whose glory, to use another of his favourite phrases, 'lies in man's truth, well-being and happiness'. It is interesting to compare Schillebeeckx with Moltmann, as one can do because volumes containing sermons by each of them have appeared almost simultaneously.[4] The two men have a great deal in common in their preaching, particularly in their understanding of the claims of the Third World and their concern for the underprivileged, the destitute and the oppressed, but with Schillebeeckx – odious though comparisons are – there is somehow an extra dimension, which comes not only from his outreach beyond Moltmann's Reformation perspective to a longer and wider tradition of the church, but also quite simply from his basic assurance that God will secure the salvation of mankind, all that men and women can hope for, even if we do not know precisely how.

One way of summing up his work would in fact be simply to use as focal points the biblical passages which he keeps quoting again and again in a variety of contexts. There is Matthew 25, the parable of the sheep and the goats, and the offering of a glass of water to the thirsty;[5] Luke 19 and Jesus' active, involved demonstration to Zacchaeus of the love of God;[6] Revelation 21 and the picture of the new Jerusalem;[7] Luke 24 and the disciples on the road to Emmaus with their hearts burning within them.[8] The way in which he has made these passages – and anyone who cares to carry on the investigation will find a great many more – his own so that they interact constantly with his own thoughts and the modern world within which they move, shows how profoundly biblical a theologian Schillebeeckx has become, without any of the narrowness that such a description can sometimes imply.

Secondly, there is a way in which, whatever criticisms of detail may be directed at his theology and the way in which it is expressed, Schillebeeckx always makes one aware of the grandeur of the enterprise on which he is engaged, the glory of God and the happiness of man. In this – as I commented in the very first chapter[9] – he is reminiscent of that other great theologian of the twentieth century, Karl Barth. Of course the differences between the two are legion, and the very worlds for which each is writing are very different too. Nevertheless, when that has been said, it does not seem to me misleading to mention them both in the same breath.

One thing which even a superficial comparison between Barth and Schillebeeckx brings out is in each case a somewhat distanced relationship to the world of academic theology, which sets them apart from the mainstream of either biblical criticism or philosophical approaches to religion. They command attention by virtue of the sheer stature of what can, not unkindly, be termed an idiosyncratic achievement, which in figures of lesser greatness would simply pass unnoticed and uncommented on. One Dutch colleague once described Schillebeeckx as 'an incomparable soloist when it comes to writing and academic work'.[10] That is more a reflection on the practitioners of much modern theology and biblical criticism rather than on Barth and Schillebeeckx, for modern theology has no room – and often, it seems, little time – for what, they argue, must be the basic source material of any account of the faith: the life and worship of the ongoing church. Academic theology can all too easily become religious studies, phenomenology of religion, comparative religion, ancient Near Eastern studies, philosophy of religion, sociology of religion, literary criticism or whatever, and because of the legacy of more than a century of this kind of fragmentation those practitioners of theology who do not carry on their work by in fact keeping within one of these sub-disciplines find themselves compelled to devote considerable thought to a variety of problems if they seek to offer a rationale in modern circumstances of precisely what is involved in doing theology and how and where it should be done.

One alternative to that is simply to get down to writing theology in the terms which seem called for by the modern situation, before God, of the church and of the world, and that in effect is what both Barth and Schillebeeckx have done. The inevitable result is a considerable degree of isolation. Within the church a concern for exploring the depths of theology quickly brings about a break with the vast majority of fellow members who have neither the time, the ability or the inclination to pursue such questions so exhaustively. Writing books makes a person 'different'. Furthermore, exploration of this kind, if done as it should be, will inevitably lead the theologian not only to think, but to see the need for changes of attitude and behaviour and structural changes within the church and the society of the time and call for his vision to be implemented. That makes theologians threats to authorities who simply want to be left alone to run church or nation in terms with which they are familiar and with which they feel that they can cope, and can even alienate them from those who have not gone as far along the way of exploration as they have. Barth in his day found himself in trouble with both his church and the government of the countries in which he lived - Switzerland as well as Germany – for the way in which his theology led him to make pronouncements on political matters, just as Schillebeeckx has proved controversial in his.

Thus isolated from the church, those concerned with theology in this way do not find it easy to feel at home in academic theology either. Though he had no reason to feel as he did, Barth over much of his life wrote to friends that he was not really a 'proper' professor, because he was not academic enough. Schillebeeckx is more than his equal in learning, and in fact is in theory much more open to discussion than Barth's distinctive position allowed him to be. He speaks about the church as it is, he affirms, in terms that can be analysed historically and in terms of psychology and sociology, and has no time for official statements which exclusively use the language of faith. However, that does not necessarily mean that those representatives of other disciplines whose concerns he takes seriously and whose language and thought patterns he is prepared to use will necessarily join in his discussion unless he is there to ask them personally.

And if they did join in the discussion, it has to be conceded, they would not necessarily find the going easy. That is because of the magisterial position which Schillebeeckx has by now quite naturally and modestly assumed. His mind and capabilities are great enough, his learning formidable enough and his stature sufficiently assured for him legitimately to concentrate on pursuing his own quest, as circumstances have in fact allowed him to do for so many years, knowing that what interests and concerns him will also interest and concern other people. But that means that inevitably the quests of other theologians, philosophers, sociologists and so on must inevitably be of lesser importance to him and it is understandable if one feels that in some situations the dialogue is likely to be more than a little one-sided.

There is an interesting pointer to this in his books. In the vast amount of material which he has written there are countless footnotes, bearing witness to the enormous number of other writings which he has read. However, direct quotation, apart from say the New Testament, Thomas Aquinas, or church documents and decrees which he happens to be analysing, is amazingly rare. It is as if everything that he reads is taken into his mind, assimilated, thought about and correlated, and then reproduced in a quite distinctive personal way in which the thoughts of those from whom he has benefitted are transformed virtually to the point where they lose their original individuality. At times this process of assimilation and transformation can let him down. English-speaking readers with some knowledge of modern analytical philosophy might care to look at the section 'Revelation, an interpretative element? Seeing as. . .

or interpreting as. . .?', in which the discussion at times does not really pass muster as a fair and accurate account of its subject-matter.[11] Indeed, one wonders, when Schillebeeckx discusses analytical philosophy, whether he has really entered fully into its world, and for that matter whether his philosophical equipment, for all his vast reading, is as strong as it should be for a completely adequate treatment of some of the subject-areas into which he ventures. Perhaps, as one theologian and philosopher of religion pointed out to me, Louvain did Schillebeeckx a disservice in dissuading him from pursuing philosophy further.

In his treatment of other authors whom he has read and also in his sympathy for, yet distance from, modern philosophy of religion, Schillebeeckx is reminiscent of another theologian who exercised a similar, if lesser, influence in the churches in the middle years of the century – though he never expressed himself in a comparable way on political questions – namely Alan Richardson. Alan Richardson occupied a not always satisfactory position midway between church and university, spending most of his life in church positions but also holding a professorial chair in theology in a secular university. He, too, adopted Schillebeeckx's distinctive practice of assimilating the views of other writers and then blending evaluation with exposition in his accounts of their views.[12]

If this approach has its disadvantages, there is no question that it can be communicated very successfully, even when, as with Schillebeeckx, the mode of presentation can often be a deterrent. Again, as we saw, because they believe that he has his priorities right and that his concerns are theirs – one might almost say, altering one of his own favourite phrases, that his cause is God's cause – as we saw earlier, those who have discovered his books will work hard to try to understand them and will even queue up at bookshops to buy new volumes when they appear (one is reminded of the way in which during the war, in exceptionally difficult publishing circumstances, pastors went to enormous lengths to get hold of the newly-published additions to Barth's *Church Dogmatics*). And that in itself is tribute enough.

There are many aspects of Schillebeeckx's theology which it has been impossible to cover in this volume, and at the very least because of that, my account of it will inevitably have been distorted.

Moreover, any survey of Schillebeeckx's work is bound to remain incomplete until the third volume of his planned trilogy and his big book on hermeneutics appear. Because of that, and because we stand so near in time to him, it would be presumptuous in a short book of this kind to attempt any detailed assessment.

However, there are some questions which cannot be passed over completely at this point. For example, there will be those who wonder how what Schillebeeckx says relates to the official teachings of his church, and whether there may not be a grain of truth in the charges which the Vatican has brought against him. As I remarked at the beginning, a good deal of publicity has been given to the views of his critics; against that it is instructive to see what Schillebeeckx has to say. For the sake of clarity I shall keep to the way in which he reconciles the contents of his *Jesus* with the famous Definition of the Council of Chalcedon from AD 451, which ever since has been the touchstone for the church's doctrine of the person of Christ. This should indicate the lines along which he approaches other matters.

Jesus, he argues, is a man who stands in a unique relationship to God. (We saw more of how he understands this unique relationship in Chapter 4). It is understandable, given the way in which Christians thought in the fourth and fifth centuries AD, and their Greek philosophical background, that they should want to provide theoretical definitions of the relationship between Jesus and God. However, it is also dangerous. The Chalcedonian Definition is indeed a dogma which guides our faith, as do other formulations, but it is expressed in terms of a specific philosophical approach, that of Middle Platonism. At that time people were concerned with the question whether Jesus was definitive salvation for men from God. Arius and his followers, against whom the Council of Nicaea (AD 325) was directed, are commonly said to have been mistaken because of the way in which they claimed that Jesus stood in a subordinate position to God. However, that was not their real failure. They failed because they did not make Jesus the definitive salvation for all men.

It is wrong, he goes on, to proclaim that 'Jesus is truly man and truly God' as a truth in itself and to separate that confession from the way in which people responded to the question of his nature and meaning in very different terms from our own. We cannot use words like 'consubstantial' any more, not because they are learned and technical terms but because their conceptuality is alien to us. But that does not mean that we have to abandon the old definitions and creeds. They may be incomprehensible, but they serve in the liturgy as a sign of remembrance, a beacon pointing us in the right direction. In the end of the day, creeds and confessions are as it were liturgical hymns, songs of praise expressed in the language and thought forms of their time.[13]

Some may wonder how Schillebeeckx can still remain a member of the Roman Catholic Church in view of his many differences with it. Here, it is interesting to compare his answer to that of Hans Küng, with whom he has been so often associated, and to see the contrast between the two men.

Küng gives his views unprompted, in a section of *On Being a Christian* called 'Why Stay?'[14] This is a difficult question, Küng says, when so many social motivations have ceased to count and the church is no longer part of the life of the nation. But it is not unimportant whether someone keeps in touch with the family or parts from it in anger and indifference. That is a reason for people and ministers to stay. They will want to attack rigid ecclesiastical traditions, the church's institutions and rules, and the arrogance of authorities enforcing their own ideas when these make it difficult to be a Christian, far less a happy Christian. But they will not want to abandon the great Christian tradition, the life of a community of faith or the moral authority which can be exercised by the true church.

People will stay because despite everything as members of the church they have a spiritual home in which they can affirm a great history; besides, there is nowhere else to go. Breaking away leads to isolation or the formation of a new institution. Those who stay in the church while criticizing it may even come to love it as never before, because it is being hurt so much, and out of this situation new good may come. He ends:

Why stay in the Church then? There is nothing wrong with its programme. And from faith we can draw *hope* that the programme, the cause of Jesus Christ himself, as hitherto, is stronger than all the mischief which has ben created in and with the Church. That is why a decisive effort in the Church is worthwhile, why also a special effort in the Church's ministry is worthwhile – despite everything. I am not staying in the Church *although* I am a Christian. It is *because* I am a Christian that I am staying in the Church.[15]

Schillebeeckx, by contrast, never directly addresses himself to this question in any of his books. His views have to be learnt from interviews that he has given to journalists when *they* have raised the question. And when he does reply, it is notable that his answer has much less of the first person about it. Whereas Küng is obviously thinking of his own position, Schillebeeckx quite naturally, as though it is the first thing that comes into his head – as it is – thinks of others. He remains a Roman Catholic because he believes that that is the true church (which does not mean that other churches are not true). He stands in the church's tradition but cannot identify himself completely with the specific form of the church. He does not feel completely at home, but where else is he to go? The tradition extending back through Christianity to Judaism is vital for the church and has to be maintained. The way in which that is done is through the community, the people, and not the theologians, who are simply there to help the church to remain on the right course. It is the people of the church who carry on the tradition and practise it.

Some may have doubts about the degree of his enthusiasm for the time of the New Testament and the early church, particularly in connection with ministry and basic communities. Some of his writing is reminiscent of the heady days when biblical scholars believed that they had discovered a halcyon world in the past, before the problems had really begun to arise. We have seen how even in the case of one individual topic, ministry, Schillebeeckx has already had to acknowledge inadequacies in his historical account and an excessive schematism, and it could be that a presentation which began from a much more detailed historical picture, not so much dominated by a perspective of twentieth-century concerns might present problems for Schillebeeckx's views as well as those of the Roman Catholic hierarchy. Church history is very complicated indeed, and treacherous where it seems to offer plausible models for the present.[16] So if one were also less positive than he is about all the features of alternative communities, it is easy to see how an alternative thesis could emerge. But as he would be the first to point out, that is a matter of the interpretation of history and has to be decided on the evidence.

However, these considerations do lead towards a fundamental complex of questions which can in a short space only be put rather tersely and bluntly. Is he right? Is what he says true? Is this the way forward?

No theologian who has covered as much ground as Schillebeeckx in his reading and writing – and it must be remembered that Schillebeeckx's voluminous published works are only the tip of the iceberg: his lecture scripts over the years must cover tens of tens of thousands of pages – can possibly be as competent in the areas outside his own speciality into which he has made forays than in those areas which fall within his own expertise. Details are bound to be wrong. Some of the theories about the New Testament which Schillebeeckx has taken over in *Jesus* and *Christ*, for example, are far from being accepted by New Testament scholars and the evidence on which they are based is far from strong. But that is an ongoing problem in scholarship anyway. One generation's 'accepted results' are the next generation's problems, and the failure of biblical critics to get beyond constantly changing approximations and hypotheses has been the despair of systematic theologians for more than a century.

So it may be that much of what Schillebeeckx has written will date quickly, just as one can already see by looking at his work over the past how in particular periods it has been dominated by specific enthusiasms which have not lasted as long as he might have expected them to when he first made his new discovery. What will not date, however, are his gift for answering the right questions and seeing how anyone within the Christian tradition today has to respond to and engage in dialogue with other writers and researchers concerned with an enormous range of widely differing subject matter, and his attempt, single-handed, to bring all his findings and possible answers to all these questions into a synthesis which is at the same time in line with the ongoing Christian tradition. We have seen his predilection for certain biblical texts; in this connection, if there is one text which he deserves to have applied to him, it is Paul's from I Corinthians 15: 'I worked harder than any of them, though it was not I, but the grace of God which is with me.'

As in the whole enterprise of theological hermeneutics, more permanent verdicts have to wait for that 'eschatological verification' of which we have seen Schillebeeckx speaking. [17] What we ought to be reduced to asking of any theologian is whether his theology is helpful to have along the way. And there again the answer in Schillebeeckx's case is obvious. Too often elsewhere in modern theology one can come to the end of a brilliant study, admire it for its academic expertise, and then wonder precisely what else is to be done with it. With Schillebeeckx one is never in any doubt about that: theology is a task of liberation, a contribution to freedom, but a freedom which is never a vague 'being free'. It is freedom to join in God's concern which is a concern for mankind, and for human happiness, fulfilment and glory. That calls for action, praxis, and there can be no resting until what needs to be done has been done.

What of Schillebeeckx's own future? Periods of ill-health and pressure of work have delayed the completion of his planned third volume beyond its promised time, but because of the way in which he works, he has a vision of it as a whole, and feels – as we have seen[18] – that all he has to do is to find the opportunity for the physical work of writing. Because he sees the direction he is going to take and the main subject-matter that he is going to cover, he can talk about his book in advance as though the manuscript were lying on the desk in his study, and since we know from elsewhere his approach to elements of this subject-matter, in theory we can discover something of what is in store. Only in theory, however; in practice there is always the likelihood of surprise, since even Schillebeeckx himself does not know quite where he will end up on his explorations.

Though the title of the new book is not yet fixed, it will be about the church, particularly in connection with the breathing of the Holy Spirit into what messianic comunities are, what they confess and what they do. Another favourite Schillebeeckx phrase, 'belief in creation' or 'creation faith' will play a major part here, as another dimension of the theme of liberation. For those who believe that God is creator of heaven and earth, creation is the beginning of the whole of liberation. A sermon on creation elaborates the implications of this further.

The transformation of the world, the development of a better and more tolerable human society and a new earth has been given over into the hands of contingent man; therefore he cannot expect God to relieve him of his problems. Precisely on the basis of a proper creation faith we cannot pass over to God what is our task in this world, given the impassable frontier (on our side) between the infinite and the finite, which puts God in his world and man in this one. Overcoming suffering and evil, wherever we may encounter them, with all possible means of science and technology, with the help of our fellow human beings, and if necessary by revolution if nothing else will avail, is our task and our burden, in a situation characterized by finitude and contingency. It is not a matter for God, except that this task is performed in his absolute presence and therefore is a human concern which is also close to his heart. . .

I believe that it is precisely the critical and productive force of authentic creation faith (as realized in Jesus) which issues in a value, inspiration and orientation, which can constantly be universalized and in this sense secularized, which is to the advantage of all people and so as it were evades the monopoly or the particularity of the religions. Christianity can never go beyond the inexhaustible potential or expectation and inspiration in creation faith. For secularity means finitude. And although non-religious secularity sees only finitude here, religious and Christian secularity sees in this finitude God's presence, which is inexhaustible because it is absolute. On this basis, to the end of days finitude or secularity will continue to be directed towards the source and ground, inspiration and orientation, which transcends all secularity, which believers call the living God, and which cannot be comprehended within any secularization. Precisely for that reason creation faith is also the foundation of prayer and mysticism.[19]

Other themes to be covered in the new book emerge from this and from Schillebeeckx's comments elsewhere. It will be critical of the church and its structures, because they are too limited for the vision of salvation and the kingdom of God. Christians have thought too much of salvation as being within the church, whereas salvation is universal. That means that God brings about his salvation in the history of the *world*, and not primarily that of the church. This salvation is thematized, expressed and celebrated in the religions of the world, but the message of salvation is not limited to them, far less to one of them, even Christianity. So yet another theme will be the relationship of Christianity to the other religions of the world and in that perspective the question of the uniqueness of Jesus.

All of which could quite conceivably give place to a fourth volume. And then there are the other works on hermeneutics and the sacraments which are high on his list of priorities. There is no shortage of projects.

If these projects are not carried out, it will be either because Schillebeeckx's physical stamina and health are not up to achieving his purpose or because his constant other activities, lecturing and travelling, being involved in *Concilium* and otherwise putting his theology into practice, forces them into the background. It is hard to see his retirement as being a relaxed one.

It will, he says, be spent in Nijmegen. At one time it was expected that on his retirement he would go back to Belgium, but he has made too many friends in Holland and is far too attached to his surroundings to want to move now.

His study in the Albertinum, on the ground floor, looks out on to a park filled with trees, grassy lawns and flowers. In the room itself, if you are fortunate enough to visit it, or in pictures taken at interviews given in it, one can see how plants also invade the house, bringing a life of their own to a place where books seem so predominant. Schillebeeckx would not be happy without them; he is not a theologian oblivious of his surroundings or of all the good things the world has to offer: it is not part of creation faith to ignore the good things that God has made. And that combination of deep thought, faith, and love of the living beauty of nature seems an appropriate combination for a great theologian. So let that be the point at which we leave him.

Except for one last parable. We saw at the start how fond Schillebeeckx is of striking illustrations and modern parables. He is the author of this particular one, but it has never appeared in print because for once it is one which he acted out rather than wrote.

He once came to stay as a guest in my home. On the morning of his departure he mysteriously went out and came back again, to go out a second time an hour or so later. When he returned, he was clutching a large bunch of quite beautiful flowers which he handed over to us as a token of thanks. His concern that thought should be extended to careful, well-considered praxis proved to have covered even this kind gesture. As we discovered later, he had gone to the florist's twice. The first time the flowers in the shop were not as fresh as he would have liked, so having ascertained that there was to be a further delivery later in the morning, he went back to ensure that the ones he bought were fresh. They lasted longer than any other bunch we have ever been given.

Bibliography

Books by Edward Schillebeeckx referred to in the text are as follows.

*De sacramentele heilseconomie: Theologische bezinning op St Thomas'
sacramentenleer in het licht van de traditie en van de hedendaagse sacra-
mentsproblematiek* I, Nelissen 1952 (no English translation)
Christ the Sacrament, Sheed and Ward 1963 (original Dutch title *Christus,
sacrament van de Godsontmoeting*, Nelissen 1959)
Mary, Mother of the Redemption, Sheed and Ward 1964 (*Maria, moeder
van de verlossing*, Nelissen 1955)
Marriage: Human Reality and Saving Mystery, Sheed and Ward 1965 (*Het
huwelijk, aardse werkelijkheid en heilsmysterie* I, Nelissen 1963)
Revelation and Theology, Sheed and Ward 1967 (*Openbaring en theologie*,
Theologische Peilingen I, Nelissen 1964)
The Eucharist, Sheed and Ward 1968 (*Christus' tegenwoordigheid in de
eucharistie*, Nelissen 1967)
God and Man, Sheed and Ward 1969 (*God en mens*, Theologische Peilingen
2, Nelissen 1965)
God the Future of Man, Sheed and Ward 1969 (there was no Dutch edition)
World and Church, Sheed and Ward 1971 (*Wereld en Kerk*, Theologische
Peilingen 3, Nelissen 1965)
The Mission of the Church, Sheed and Ward 1973 (*De Zending van de kerk*,
Theologische Peilingen 4, Nelissen 1968)
The Understanding of Faith, Sheed and Ward 1974 (*Geloofsverstaan:
Interpretatie en Kritiek*, Theologische Peilingen 5, Nelissen 1972)
Jesus: An Experiment in Christology, Collins and Crossroad Publishing Co,
New York 1979 (*Jezus, het verhaal van een levende*, Nelissen 1974)
Christ: The Christian Experience in the Modern World, SCM Press 1980
(US title *Christ: The Experience of Jesus as Lord*, Crossroad Publishing
Co 1980: *Gerechtigheid en liefde: Genade en bevrijding*, Nelissen 1977)
Interim Report on the Books Jesus *and* Christ, SCM Press and Crossroad
Publishing Co 1980 (*Tussentijds verhaal over twee Jezusboeken*, Nelissen
1978)
Ministry: A Case for Change, SCM Press 1981 (US Title, *Ministry: Lead-*

ership in the Community of Jesus Christ, Crossroad Publishing Co 1981:
Kerkelijk ambt: Voorgangers in de gemeente van Jezus Christus, Nelissen
1980)
God Among Us: The Gospel Proclaimed, SCM Press and Crossroad
Publishing Co 1983 (*Evangelie verhalen*, Nelissen 1982)
Theologisch Geloofsverstaan Anno 1983, Nelissen 1983 (English translation
forthcoming)

Also:

God is ieder ogenblik nieuw, gesprekken met Edward Schillebeeckx, by
Huub Oosterhuis and Piet Hoogeveen, Amboboeken, Baarn 1982 (translation forthcoming)
Meedenken met Edward Schillebeeckx, ed. Hermann Häring, Ted Schoof
and Ad Willems, Nelissen, Baarn 1983

For the complete bibliography of Schillebeeckx's works, see *Tijdschrift
voor Theologie* 14, 1974, 491-501 (for works up to that date); some additional
pre-1974 writings and a bibliography from 1974 to 1982 are given in
Meedenken met Edward Schillebeeckx, pp.320-325. Details of Schillebeeckx's unpublished lectures are to be found in Ted Schoofs, '. . .een bijna
koorstachtige aandrang', in the same volume, pp. 11-39.

Notes

1. Introduction

Bibliographical details of the works of Schillebeeckx mentioned in the notes, including *God is ieder ogenblik nieuw* and *Meedenken met Edward Schillebeeckx*, are given in the Bibliography.

1. *God is ieder ogenblik nieuw*, p.153.
2. *Jesus*, pp.17f.
3. *Jesus*, p.674.
4. *Christ the Sacrament*, p.77.
5. Interview with Ton Oostveen, *De Tijd*, 21 December 1979, p.77.
6. See below, pp.104ff.
7. *Christ*, pp.847ff.
8. *God is ieder ogenblik nieuw*, pp.156f.
9. *God is ieder ogenblik nieuw*, p.154.
10. See below, pp.117ff.
11. For full details of publishers and original Dutch titles see the Bibliography.
12. 'The Sacraments, An Encounter with God', in *Christianity Divided*, ed. Daniel J.Callahan, Heiko A.Oberman and Daniel J. O'Hanlon, Sheed and Ward 1962, pp.245-70.
13. See Ted Schoof, '. . .een bijna koortsachtige aandrang', in *Meedenken met Edward Schillebeeckx*, pp.14, 38.
14. *Jesus*, pp.34f.
15. *The Eucharist*, p.25.
16. G. F. Woods, 'Doctrinal Criticism', in *Prospect for Theology*, ed. F. G. Healey, Nisbet 1966, pp.73-92; cf. M. F. Wiles, *The Remaking of Christian Doctrine*, SCM Press 1974; *Working Papers in Doctrine*, SCM Press 1976.
17. *Interim Report*, p.89.
18. *Interim Report*, p.1.
19. See below, pp.88f.
20. See Ted Schoof, '. . .een bijna koortsachtige aandrang', p.38.
21. Mark (Ted) Schoof, *Breakthrough*, Gill and Macmillan 1970, p.141.

22. See Ted Schoof, '. . .een bijna koortsachtige aandrang', p.11.
23. See below, pp.88f., 149f.

2. Life

1. For the information in this chapter I am particularly indebted to various interviews given by Edward Schillebeeckx: for the early years especially G. Puchinger, in *Ro: Maandblad Reünisten Organisatie Societas Studiosorum Reformatorum*, May 1974, pp.3–41; also 'De verkettering van Edward Schillebeeckx', by Frits Groeneweld and Klaas van Gelder, in *NRC Handelsblad*, 10 November 1979, and *God is ieder ogenblik nieuw*.
2. M. D. Chenu, *Informations catholiques internationales 233*, 1 February 1965, p.30, quoted in Schoof, *Breakthrough*, p.104.
3. 'Dominican Spirituality', in *God among Us*, pp.232-48.
4. See Ted Schoof, '. . .een bijna koortsachtige aandrang', p.16.
5. *Concilium* is published in Britain by T. & T. Clark and in the United States by Seabury Press.
6. Groeneweld and van Gelder, *NRC Handelsblad*.
7. See below, p.118.
8. See below, p.83.
9. See below, pp.130ff.
10. See below, p.76.
11. Quoted in *God among Us*, p.250.
12. *Theologisch Geloofsverstaan Anno 1983,* p.3.

3. Christ the Sacrament

1. See below, pp.83ff.
2. 'The Sacraments, an Encounter with God', pp.248f.
3. *Christ the Sacrament*, p.42.
4. 'The Sacraments, an Encounter with God', p.252.
5. *Christ the Sacrament*, p.54.
6. *Christ the Sacrament*, p.68.
7. *Christ the Sacrament*, p.67.
8. *Christ the Sacrament*, p.73.
9. See above, pp.4f.
10. *Christ the Sacrament*, p.77.
11. *Christ the Sacrament*, p.119.
12. *Christ the Sacrament*, p.222.
13. *The Eucharist*, pp.16f.
14. See p.13 above.

4. Jesus

1. Albert Schweitzer, *The Quest of the Historical Jesus*, A. & C. Black ³1954; for a continuation of the account into the twentieth century see John H. Hayes, *Son of God to Superstar*, Abingdon Press, Nashville 1976.

2. See H. G. Reventlow, *Bibelautorität und Geist der Moderne*, Vandenhoeck and Ruprecht 1980.

3. H. S. Reimarus, *Fragments*, ET SCM Press and Fortress Press 1971.

4. See especially *Jesus and the Word*, Scribner, New York 1954 and Fontana Books 1958; *Theology of the New Testament* 1, Scribner, New York, and SCM Press 1951.

5. *Jesus*, p.56.

6. *Jesus*, p.57.

7. *Jesus*, p.143.

8. *Jesus*, pp.266f.

9. *Jesus*, p.380.

10. *Jesus*, p.391.

11. *Interim Report*, pp.74ff.; cf. *Jesus*, pp.644-50.

12. See e.g. Peter Selby, *Look for the Living*, SCM Press 1976; C. F. Evans, *Resurrection and the New Testament*, SCM Press 1970, and the books discussed there.

13. *Interim Report*, pp.80f.

14. *Interim Report*, p.67.

15. Ernst Käsemann, *New Testament Questions of Today*, SCM Press and Fortress Press 1969, p.137.

16. *Interim Report*, p.71.

17. *Interim Report*, pp.98f.

18. See above, pp.2, 35.

19. Ted Schoof, '. . .een bijna koortsachtige aandrang'.

20. See below, pp.130f.

21. His last major book had been *Marriage* (see Bibliography).

5. Ministry

1. See especially Jan Kerkhofs, 'From Frustration to Liberation', in *Minister, Pastor, Prophet*, SCM Press and Crossroad Publishing Co 1980, pp.5ff.

2. 'From Frustration to Liberation', pp.6-10.

3. *Ministry*, p.vi.

4. *Ministry*, p.5.

5. *Ministry*, p.33.

6. *Ministry*, p.41.

7. Graham Greene, e.g. *The Power and the Glory*, Heinemann 1940, reissued Penguin Books 1962.

8. *Ministry*, p.64.

9. *Ministry*, p.114.

10. *Ministry*, p.142.

11. 'De sociale context van de verschuivingen in het kerkelijk ambt', *Tijdschrift voor Theologie* 22, 1982, pp.24-59.

6. Salvation from God

1. *Christ*, p.33.
2. Ibid.
3. *Interim Report*, pp.13f.
4. Julian of Norwich, *Revelations of Divine Love*, Chapters 5,32, Penguin Books 1966, pp.68, 109.
5. Peter Berger, *A Rumour of Angels*, Allen Lane The Penguin Press 1970, pp.72f.
6. *God is ieder ogenblik nieuw*, p.133.
7. *Christ*, p.725.
8. *God is ieder ogenblik nieuw*, p.135.
9. He has made this point often; this particular way of putting it comes from an interview in *Hervormd Nederland*, 4 September 1982, p.4.
10. See above, pp.55ff.
11. *Christ*, p.743.

7. Spirituality

1. See above, p.14.
2. *God Among Us*, pp.225-31.
3. *God Among Us*, pp.194-8.
4. *God Among Us*, p 196.
5. *God Among Us*, p.232.
6. *God Among Us*, pp.235f.
7. See above, pp.29f.
8. *God Among Us*, pp.244f.
9. *God Among Us*, pp.245f.
10. See above, p.6.

8. Political Theology

1. L. Bessières, *Les acrobates de Dieu*, Paris 1975, pp.32f., quoted in *God Among Us*, pp.197f.
2. *God is ieder ogenblik nieuw*, p.117.
3. Fernando Belo, *A Materialist Interpretation of the Gospel of Mark*, Orbis Books, Maryknoll 1981.
4. J. P. Miranda, *Marx and the Bible*, Orbis Books 1973 and SCM Press 1977.
5. *God is ieder ogenblik nieuw*, p.121.
6. M. Rostovtzeff, *The Social and Economic History of the Hellenistic World*, Vols I-III, Oxford University Press 1941.
7. Oscar Cullmann, *Jesus and the Revolutionaries of his Time*, Harper and Row, New York 1970; Martin Hengel, *Was Jesus a Revolutionist?*, Fortress Press, Philadelphia 1971.
8. *Christ*, pp.568ff.

9. *Christ*, p.559.

10. *God Among Us*, pp. 59-62.

11. *God is ieder ogenblik nieuw*, p.47; Schillebeeckx repeated the point in an interview in *The Observer*, 20 February 1983, p.3.

12. Gustavo Gutierrez, *Theology of Liberation*, Orbis Books 1973 and SCM Press 1974.

13. *Christ*, p.514.

14. *God Among Us*, p.170.

15. *God Among Us*, p.172.

16. *Ministry*, pp.131-4.

17. For what follows see especially *God is ieder ogenblik nieuw*, pp.93ff.

9. *'A Brief Hermeneutical Intermezzo'*

1. *Ministry*, pp.100-4.

2. *Ministry*, p.101.

3. *Ministry*, p.104.

4. See Ted Schoofs, '. . .een bijna koortsachtige aandrang', p.24.

5. Ibid., p.30.

6. See above, p.35.

7. *Theologisch Geloofsverstaan Anno 1983*, Nelissen, Baarn 1983.

8. *Theologisch Geloofsverstaan*, pp.17f.

9. *Theologisch Geloofsverstaan*, p.7.

10. Posed e.g. in *For Faith and Freedom* Vol.II, Blackwell 1957, pp.15f.

11. Leonard Hodgson, *Sex and Christian Freedom*, SCM Press 1967, p.42; quoted by D.E.Nineham, *The Use and Abuse of the Bible*, Macmillan 1976, p.175, who has a good discussion of the point.

12. *The Understanding of Faith*, pp.58f.

13. *The Understanding of Faith*, p.62.

14. *Theologisch Geloofsverstaan*, p.16.

15. Ted Schoof, 'Masters in Israel: VII. The Later Theology of Edward Schillebeecckx', *The Clergy Review*, 55, 1970, p.952.

10. *Assessment – and the Future*

1. These comments were made by John Whale in *The Sunday Times*, 6 February 1983, in a review of Graham Shaw, *The Cost of Authority*, SCM Press 1983, which he put in the former category.

2. Don Cupitt, *The World to Come*, SCM Press 1982, Chapter 1.

3. *Theologisch Geloofsverstaan*, p. 21.

4. Jürgen Moltmann, *The Power of the Powerless*, SCM Press and Harper and Row, San Francisco 1983, and *God Among Us*.

5. See above, p.121.

6. See above, p.135.

7. See above, p.99.

8. See above, p.49.

9. See above, p.3.

10. W. Grossouw, *Alles is van u*, Baarn 1981, p.276, quoted in Ted Schoof, 'een bijna koortsachtige aandrang'.

11. See *Christ*, pp.49ff.

12. See especially *The Bible in the Age of Science*, SCM Press 1961.

13. *God is ieder ogenblik nieuw*, pp.59ff.

14. Hans Küng, *On Being a Christian*, Doubleday, New York and Collins 1977, pp.522-5.

15. Ibid., p.525.

16. See especially D. E. Nineham, *The Use and Abuse of the Bible*; Robert L. Wilken, *The Myth of Christian Beginnings*, Doubleday, New York 1971, reissued SCM Press 1979.

17. See above, pp.137f.

18. See above, p.118.

19. *God Among Us*, p.96.

Index

Adam, Karl, 26, 28
Albertinum, 32, 108, 153
Alfrink, Cardinal, 34
Apostles, 77f.
Apostolic succession, 79
Albertus Magnus, 14, 25, 30, 105–7, 112, 113
Aquinas, Thomas, 25, 27, 50, 105, 107, 112, 131f., 145
Augustine, 41, 45, 82, 128
Auschwitz, 95

Barth, Karl, 3, 143–6
Basic communities, 83, 87, 118, 149
Belo, F., 119
Berger, P., 93
Brand, P., 34
Buber, M., 3, 36

Camus, A., 30, 101
Celibacy, 77, 81, 86
Chalcedon, Council of, 71, 81, 105, 147
Chenu, M. D., 14, 28, 29, 30f., 113
Christ, 3, 8, 9, 10, 11, 14, 15, 16, 18, 20, 27, 61, 68, 72, 73, 91, 94, 98, 102, 150
Christ the Sacrament, 1, 2, 4, 6, 7, 9, 10, 139ff.
Clichtove, Josse, 81
Concelebration, 82
Concilium, 34, 153
Congar, Yves, 29, 113
Conversion process, 64, 65, 66f.
Correlation, 124
Creation faith, 17, 151f.
Critical theory, 7, 34
Cyprian, 80f.

Dispensation, principle of, 112
Doctrinal criticism, 13f., 51
Dominic, St , 105, 110, 111, 113
Dominican spirituality, 105–116
Dominican sisters, 115
Dominicans, 6, 24ff., 29ff.

Eckhardt, Meister, 25, 112
Encounter, 6, 41, 45, 46, 48, 50
Enlightenment, 12, 56, 101
Erasmus prize, 6, 8, 36
Eschatological prophet, 17, 68, 69f.
Eschatological verification, 137
Eucharist, 6, 39f., 77, 80, 84
Eucharist, The, 7, 9, 13, 50f.
Existentialism, 2, 6, 40
Experience, 11, 27, 41, 43, 60, 65, 78, 91f., 95, 96, 98f.
Experiences of contrast, 92, 100

Feminist theology, 127f.
Frankfurt School, 7, 34, 133

Galileo, 140
Gilson, Etienne, 29
God, 17, 19, 22, 37, 41ff., 48, 59, 62ff., 92f., 95f., 98, 102, 113, 115f., 124f., 127, 131, 136ff., 143, 151ff.
  as creator, 5, 96
Grace, 11, 41, 42, 46, 65, 72, 123
Greene, Graham, 83
Gutierrez, G., 122

Habermas, J., 3, 132
Hermeneutics, 7, 9, 35, 38, 72, 130–40, 147
Hick, J., 137
Hodgson, L., 136
Honest to God, 7, 141
Hope, 101, 142

Ideology, 77, 97, 134
Incarnation, 96
India, 23f.
Interim Report, 8, 9, 14, 16, 65, 68, 91

Jesuits, 23, 24f.
Jesus, 1, 2, 3, 7f., 9, 10, 11, 13, 14, 15, 16, 17, 18, 20, 36, 54, 55ff., 57ff., 98, 130, 132, 142, 147, 150
Jesus, historical, 13ff.

importance of, 35, 96f.
Jordan of Saxony, 105f.
Julian of Norwich, 93

King, Martin Luther, 122
Kingdom of God, 4, 9, 17, 34, 41, 58,
   61, 62, 68, 70, 75, 97, 109, 121, 124
Küng, H., 2, 6, 148, 149

Lacordaire, H. D., 25, 112, 113
Latin American priests, letter of, 76,
   125f.
Liberation, liberation theology, 34,
   37, 94, 118, 122ff.

*Marriage: Human Reality and Saving
   Mystery*, 7, 132
Mary, Mother of the Redemption, 7,
   115
Marx, Marxism, 12, 17, 30, 119
Ministry, 40, 45, 74ff., 149
Ministry, 8, 9, 16, 18, 36, 74–89, 125,
   130
Miranda, J. P., 119
Moltmann, J., 142f.
Mysticism, mystics, 25, 124f., 152

Narrative theology, 134f.
Newman, J. H., 139
New Testament, 11, 13, 14, 35, 55,
   57, 60f., 63, 67f., 79f., 80, 91, 98,
   99, 119, 123, 137, 145, 149, 150
Nicaea, Council of, 86, 105, 147
Nuclear power, 36

Old Testament, 13, 29, 69, 80f., 86
Ordinatio, 81, 84

Petter, D., ed, 26, 27, 28, 31
Philosophy, 12, 13, 27, 132, 145
Pico della Mirandola, G., 37
Political theology, 6, 9, 29, 103, 115,
   117–29
Praxis, 4, 5, 6, 62f., 95, 109, 127, 137,
   140, 151
Prayer, 6, 25, 95
Proportionality, 138f.

Reimarus, H. S., 57, 120
Resurrection, 43, 49, 63ff., 68, 70, 72,
   98f.
Revelation, 42, 92, 128
Richardson, A., 146
Right to ministers, 76, 80
Roman law, 84
Romero, Oscar, 95, 127

Sacrament, primordial, 43, 44, 45
Sacramentele heilseconomie, De, 16,
   40
Salvation, 17, 45, 59, 60, 67, 70, 72,
   92, 93, 97, 99–103, 147, 152
Saulchoir, Le, 29, 30
Savonarola, G., 112
Schillebeeckx, Constant Johannes
   (father), 21, 22, 25f.
Schillebeeckx, Johanna Petronella
   (mother), 21, 22
Second innocence, 56, 58
Spirituality, 9, 31, 54, 104–16
Suffering, 94f., 152
Synod of Bishops 1971, 87
Synthesis, 12, 101, 140, 150

Tertullian, 82
Third World, 6, 34, 36, 118, 125, 135,
   142
Transsubstantiation, 13, 40, 50, 51,
   52f.
Trent, Council of, 7, 46, 50, 51, 52,
   81, 82, 84, 87, 132
Twelve, The, 77f.

Understanding of Faith, The, 7, 132,
   137
Utopia, 12, 94

Vatican II, 1, 32ff., 35, 38, 77, 81, 85,
   110, 132
Violence, 121
Voillaume, R., 31

Wiles, M. F., 14
Willebrands, Cardinal, 34
Women, ordination of, 86
Woods, G. F., 14
Worship, 45, 46